Small Practice
and the Sole Practitioner

Marianne Davys

RIBA  **Publishing**

© RIBA Publishing, 2017

Published by RIBA Publishing, part of RIBA Enterprises Ltd,
The Old Post Office, St Nicholas Street, Newcastle upon Tyne, NE1 1RH

ISBN 978-1-85946-725-1

The right of Marianne Davys to be identified as the Author of this Work has
been asserted in accordance with the Copyright, Designs and Patents Act 1988
sections 77 and 78.

British Library Cataloguing-in-Publication Data

A catalogue record for this book is available from the British Library.

Commissioning Editor: Elizabeth Webster
Project Editor: Daniel Culver
Production: Michèle Woodger
Designed & Typeset by Mercer Design, London
Printed and bound by WG Baird
Cover designed by Philip Handley
Cover image: Springfield Ave. N10. Tim Crocker/Marianne Davys

While every effort has been made to check the accuracy and quality of the
information given in this publication, neither the Author nor the Publisher
accept any responsibility for the subsequent use of this information, for
any errors or omissions that it may contain, or for any misunderstandings
arising from it.

www.ribaenterprises.com

CONTENTS

INTRODUCTION

This book is written for architects who are thinking of setting up a small practice or working as sole practitioners. There are between 9000 and 12000 architectural practices in the UK – estimates vary. Around 79% of RIBA Chartered Practices employ fewer than 10 people, according to the 2017 RIBA Business Benchmarking Survey.[1]

The book will be of interest to existing sole practitioners, architects thinking of setting up a small practice or already running a small practice, and to Part II or Part III students who would like to set up in practice themselves, or work for a small practice or on small projects at some point in their career.

Architectural courses, despite their length, give little or no guidance on setting up and running a business. This book, in three separate parts, will aim to do just that. At the end of the book, there are 10 case studies of the typical kinds of projects that a small practice or sole practitioner might take on.

▷ PART 1: SETTING UP A SMALL ARCHITECTURAL PRACTICE

▷ PART 2: SMALL PRACTICE MANAGEMENT

▷ PART 3: SMALL PROJECT MANAGEMENT

Detailed advice on setting up a new practice is already available in books from the RIBA Bookshop or online.[2] Guidance on practice and project management is also available. However, much of the guidance is aimed at architectural practices of any size, undertaking projects of any size, so it can be difficult to decide how to scale down the administration and the recommended procedures when working at a smaller scale. This aspect will be covered in more detail throughout the book.

One of the challenges for any small practice is working with domestic clients, or clients who have not worked with architects before, who do not know what to expect from their architect. Clients might be stressed about finances or builders working in their home, so if you chose to work with domestic clients you must find ways to make their experience as enjoyable as possible, and you need to be prepared to explain exactly what architects do. The advantages and disadvantages of working with domestic clients will be covered in detail in Part 2.

Another challenge is working on small projects without a quantity surveyor, and providing your clients with accurate cost information. Advice on this topic is included in Part 3.

Probably the biggest challenge for the small practice is to take on small but complex projects, provide a professional service, deliver projects that are well designed and detailed, work within budget, meet clients' expectations – and at the same time generate a reasonable profit. This is not easy: generally, the smaller the project the harder it is to make a profit. Tips and advice on this topic are included in Parts 2 and 3.

Case studies of typical small projects (£50,000 to £750,000) showing the challenges they present are included at the end of the book.

References in this book to tax, insurance, legislation, company law, regulations and codes of practice are current at the time of going to press, but changes and revisions are frequent so check online that you are following current guidance.

ABOUT THE AUTHOR

Marianne Davys is an architect and sole director of Marianne Davys Architects Ltd, established in 1999 and which focuses on domestic projects, small commercial projects and work for private schools.

Marianne has wide experience of design and delivery in both the public and the private sector. She has delivered planning permissions on sensitive sites and has expertise in the management and coordination of multi-disciplinary consultant teams through all project stages.

She has sat on various RIBA committees and panels including the RIBA Small Practice Committee and the Guerilla Tactics sub-committee, the RIBA Plan of Work and the BIM review groups.

She lectures annually at the Cambridge School of Architecture to RIBA Part III students on setting up and running a small architectural practice.

Marianne lives and works in North London in the house she has extended and modified to accommodate her practice and the different stages of family life.

THE AUTHOR WOULD LIKE TO EXTEND HER THANKS:

To the Senior Commissioning Editor Liz Webster, for her suggestion that the book should be written and her support, encouragement and patience working with a first time author, and to the whole team at RIBA Publishing.

To Nigel Ostime for his encouragement, advice and support from the day the book was first mentioned through to publication.

To the small practices who have contributed case studies and the photographers who have given permission to use their photographs in the book.

To Adrian Dobson, Maureen Diffley, Robert Davys, Bob Batey and Kathleen Morrison for their comments and endorsements, to Jeremy Poulter and Steve Townsend for their advice on BIM and CDM, and to Philippa Worke, Paul Vonberg, Chris Hunt and Dennis Hellyar for their reviews.

To Sarah Baxter at the Society of Authors who provided guidance on being an author.

To my daughter Emma who inspired the idea of running a small architectural practice from a home office and who was always there to provide moral support.

> # Part 1
> ## Setting up a small architectural practice

CONTEXT

What is a 'small practice'?

The RIBA defines small practices as those that employ between 6 and 10 people, and micropractices as those that employ between 2 and 5 people. A huge number of practices fall into this category, and the range of projects on which they work is extensive.

This book will mainly focus on the very small or micropractice, as well as the sole practitioner architect operating from a home office and taking on relatively small projects. As well as architects, structural engineers, quantity surveyors, VAT consultants and party wall surveyors can all work successfully as sole practitioners.

Company structure

Once you have decided whether you are going to work on your own or with others, how many people you would like to employ, where you will be based, the type and size of project you prefer, the turnover you hope to achieve, and how much capital you can access, you can then decide what type of company structure is best suited to your needs, taking into account the advantages and disadvantages of the different options. For more detail on company structure, see pages 33–35.

Management structure

The sole practitioner architect will do everything in the office – from tasks requiring skill and experience such as bringing in work, running projects, IT, and managing finances, to the simplest of tasks such as changing the ink in the photocopier, going to the post office or ordering stationery. For this reason a sole practitioner must be organised and efficient to avoid spending a disproportionate amount of time on admin, which would negatively affect the practice income.

THE SOLE PRACTITIONER WHO RUNS A SMALL HOME
OFFICE WILL HAVE A DIFFERENT WORKING DAY FROM A
PARTNER IN A LARGER PRACTICE. SOME ARCHITECTS MIGHT
PERFORM BRILLIANTLY IN A LARGE PRACTICE BUT FIND
THE CHALLENGES OF A SMALL PRACTICE IMPOSSIBLE TO
MANAGE, AND VICE VERSA.

Architects choose to operate at a small scale for a variety of reasons, including being able to work from a home office, or they might simply enjoy working on small projects with domestic clients. If a small practice is well set up and professionally run, the practice should be able to grow to five or more members with ease if growth is an objective.

With four or five people in the office a more formal management structure and office accommodation will be necessary, but there is also more scope for employing staff with a range of qualifications, experience and skill. Apart from one or two senior architects, the office might employ a Part I or Part II architect, an architectural assistant, an office manager or an interior designer.

Turnover

A sole practitioner with low overheads and working from a home office might only have to do between £600k–£1m worth of construction work, spread over a number of projects, to generate sufficient turnover to run the practice successfully and earn a reasonable salary (comparable to what an architect would earn in a larger practice). With, say, five staff a practice can take on a wider range of projects and larger projects but would have much higher overheads, including the cost of renting office premises, so would have to bring in significantly more fee income per architect than the sole practitioner working from a home office.

A small practice might decide to run three or four projects rather than one project of the necessary value, for less risk in terms of turnover and cashflow. However, jobs that are too small may not be viable, so it is important to establish what size and type of job is right for your practice and only take on larger or smaller projects after careful consideration.

Profit

The profit made by the practice will depend on bringing in enough work, charging the right fee for each project, the overheads, and how much employees are paid. In cities like London there is a lot of work that can be done by small offices and sole practitioners, and the fees are likely to be higher than elsewhere in the UK, but overheads and the cost of living are also higher.

Whatever the size of the practice – whether one person or five, whether in your attic or in commercial premises in Central London – to be successful it must be set up and run as a business with appropriate management structure, systems and procedures to deliver a professional service. Every practice must achieve a balance between fee income and company overheads and generate a profit in order to survive and thrive.

Small practice projects

Projects for private domestic clients are the main but not the only source of work for sole practitioners and small practices. Within the domestic category projects will vary significantly in value, and there are numerous sub-categories, some of which will require specialist skills – such as the skills of a conservation architect.

Examples of small practice projects

RESIDENTIAL WORK

- works to privately-owned Grade I-listed houses
- works to privately-owned Grade II-listed houses or apartments in conservation areas, including extensions, refurbishment and alterations
- works to existing privately-owned houses and apartments
- new private houses.

COMMERCIAL WORK

- alterations and extensions to existing commercial buildings
- small housing developments
- doctors' surgeries
- shops
- private schools
- stables and farm buildings
- restaurants
- galleries
- offices and studios
- interiors
- exhibition stands
- buy-to-let properties or domestic rental properties
- housing Association projects
- work on existing churches including Grade I - or II - listed churches
- work as a subconsultant to another firm of architects for a specific project
- work for a developer.

Larger projects

Working on large commercial projects, government projects, and Housing Association and local authority projects is possible, but might not be right for the sole practitioner or small practice unless it is set up to do this type of work. There is a risk associated with taking on one large project rather than a few smaller ones: the big job might fall through, and any late payment of fees could cause cashflow problems. You might also have to do some preliminary work for no fee and no guarantee that you will be appointed for the whole project. The methods used for the procurement of consultants usually rule out very small practices on the grounds that they will not have the relevant experience or enough professional indemnity cover, even though a small practice will often have the ability, the resources and the technical skill to do the project.

Work from outside the UK

Working outside the UK is becoming more common, with the increase in digital communication and collaboration, but a small practice should carefully consider whether such a project will be financially viable, especially if there will be a lot of time spent on site. The logistics of building far away from the office become more difficult to manage the smaller the project is. Construction law, and Planning and Building Regulations also vary from one country to another – even between Scotland and England. A good rule of thumb is that the smaller the project, the closer to the office it should be, unless the fee has been carefully calculated to ensure that travel time and any other expenses are covered. Additional professional indemnity (PI) insurance may also be required to cover a project outside the UK.

Other work

Work that can also bring in income and provide an important source of new contacts includes the following:

- teaching at architecture schools
- lecturing to Part III students
- speaking at conferences
- principal designer duties under the CDM Regulations (in detail in Part 3).

Specialisation

Specialisms – such as interior design skills, being a registered Conservation Architect or having expertise in a particular area of work such as doctors' surgeries or the refurbishment of domestic properties – can be a good way of bringing in work, via a portfolio of relevant completed projects on the practice website.

Existing projects

With domestic work, existing projects are a great source of more work. Clients will often set a budget lower than is realistic for the project they actually want, as they are concerned about costs they will not be able to control. As a project develops and the client starts to relax and trust the team, they will often ask the architect to add extra work to the project. These late-stage requests to do more work can be time-consuming to deal with, so you need to ensure that extra resources are always available. However, this work can be quite lucrative if your fee is a fixed percentage based on the final contract value.

Know when to say no

It is important to know what types of projects and values are right for your practice, and to be confident that you have the skills and resources to deal with a project. It is equally important to know when a project or a client is not right for the practice and to be able to say no. To not get a desired job is unfortunate, but to take on the wrong project, or the wrong client, can be disastrous – and could potentially ruin a small practice that might otherwise have been successful.

You will put a lot of effort into bringing in work, and your success as a business will depend on this, but it is also important not to take on too much work relative to the resources available. Resources should always be available for the project you really want to do that unexpectedly comes into the office, or for additional work on an existing project. Taking on extra staff to increase resources is possible, but the implications for the practice need to be carefully considered in advance.

The value of experience before setting up a practice

The more experience, contacts and skills you have acquired, or can acquire, the easier the process of setting up a new architectural practice will be. Despite the huge number of sole practitioners and small practices, there is little or no part of an architectural education that prepares the architect to run their own business. In most cases, unless the necessary skills have been acquired by working for others, some form of business training as well as financial advice and legal advice will be essential.

Much can be learned by working in at least a few architectural practices of varying type and size and understanding and contributing to how they are set up and managed. Some practices will be well set up, with systems in place to allow for growth, while others will be less well organised. Helping an existing practice to improve is a good way of clocking up experience that can be used later in setting up your own practice.

Before setting up in practice you must be sure you have acquired the skills necessary to run the projects that will come into the office, as well as those needed to set up and run a business. One of the most important is being able to understand cashflow: what money is coming in and what money is going out. Where such skills are lacking, they should be bought in and not just learned on the job.

Before setting up my own practice I had worked in the public and private sectors on a range of projects, from small refurbishments to large local authority projects. I had developed a good understanding of the Building Regulations and the construction industry in the UK, and how a range of architectural practices were run and managed. I had gained experience of the type of project our new practice would undertake, which is mostly residential work with a strong emphasis on the refurbishment of period and listed properties. Without this experience and a network of contacts, it would have been much harder to bring in work in the early years. There are, however, many successful large and small practices that were set up by architects early in their careers – so it is possible with help and hard work, but the more experience and contacts you have first, the easier it will be.

Go at your own pace

It is a lot easier and requires less skill to run two small jobs at the same time than five small jobs at the same time. When starting out in practice and doing everything for the first time, everything will take longer. Starting slowly and gradually building up the workload and the pace will allow you to take on more work as all the office systems and network of contacts become established.

Mentoring

If you are young and have limited experience and only a small network of contacts, you might be able to approach a more established practice that does similar work to mentor you through the first year or two of your new practice. This could be an invaluable source of advice: older architects have the edge when it comes to experience, knowledge and contacts, while younger architects tend to have boundless energy and no problems with IT and social media, so an exchange of skills between a fledgling and an established practice might benefit both.

Advice from colleagues

You should be able to get good advice from architect colleagues already running their own small practices. You can also get advice from an accountant – especially if they work for other small architectural practices – a bookkeeper, a quantity surveyor or a structural engineer.

Contacts

The people you know, and in particular those you have worked with in the construction industry, will be good sources of new work. This might include referrals from architects you have worked with previously, but it could also be clients, structural engineers, quantity surveyors, VAT consultants or contractors. Make sure everybody knows that you are setting up a small practice, especially if you are specialising in domestic work, as everyone you meet is a potential client.

Business training

Whatever level of experience you have as an architect, the task of setting up a practice will be challenging. A full understanding of what is involved is essential, gained through advice from colleagues and other professionals, research and training. If the plan is to set up as a small practice and stay small, that will require one approach. If the plan is to set up as a small practice and to grow as quickly as possible, the growth plan should be accommodated from day one. Once the practice becomes busy it will be hard to find the time to move office or change the structure of your company.

If you decide that you do not have the business skills necessary to set up and run your business, try to find a short course in business training that is local and at a time that suits you, as you will probably still be working full-time as an employee architect. Details of courses provided by local colleges can be found online.

Networking

Once you have set up the practice, networking with other practices similar to your own will provide crucial support. You will be able to share CPD seminars, talk over problems or ask for advice – sometimes just ask for a second opinion; share contractors, photographers, website designers or IT support, arrange holiday or illness cover; and so on. For the sole practitioner this network of colleagues is the next best thing to having more senior people in your own office.

The RIBA Small Practice Committee arranges a popular annual conference at the RIBA called Guerilla Tactics. This is a good opportunity to catch up on CPD and to network with other small practices. You will find that the questions raised by delegates are often about the same issues your practice faces. A question raised during a session can often be followed up by an interesting chat during the next coffee break.

SETTING UP

Setting up a new practice

Architects are not trained to set up and run small businesses, so the necessary skills must be acquired by extra training while working for someone else, or bought in from outside, or a combination of both. Remember that the decision to set up an architectural practice does not have to be made quickly. The idea can gradually develop as you gather all the necessary information to know what is involved before making the decision to proceed. You can also continue to earn a salary while employed elsewhere, and build up some capital while the idea of the new practice develops.

If the practice is going to be small – perhaps one or two people working in a home office on domestic projects – the logistics of setting up will be easier and the capital required significantly less than for a new practice with, say, three to five staff based in commercial premises hoping to take on large projects and to grow quickly. No two practices will be set up or run in exactly the same way, but there are basic, core requirements that must be met by all practices so they operate in accordance with the ARB Architects Code: Standards of Conduct and Practice, and as successful businesses, no matter what size they are.

Technology and digital communication now make it possible to operate a small practice at a professional level with little more than one person and a laptop – however, that person must have all the skills necessary to run a successful business, and those skills have not changed since the days of drawing boards and T-squares.

Setting up a new practice can be broken down into four separate stages, with the level of commitment required increasing at each stage.

▷ STAGE 1: Questions, conversations and research

▷ STAGE 2: Decisions

▷ STAGE 3: Setting up

▷ STAGE 4: Ready to trade

▷ **STAGE 1:** Questions, conversations and research

At this stage the new practice is just an idea in your head or a chat in the pub after work. You are not spending any money, and no decisions are final. At the end of this stage you may have nothing on paper but you will either have decided against the idea, or to take it to the next stage.

Here are some questions before proceeding to the next stage:

- Why are you doing this: to have more control over the projects you design? To make money? To become famous? To be able to work from home? For family reasons? To improve your quality of life?
- Are you going to do this alone, or with others?
- Are you going to employ staff?
- Are you going to work full-time?
- Have you got some capital?
- Are you prepared for the financial risks of a new business?
- Can you cope with financial insecurity?
- Can you deal with stress positively?
- If the business struggles, will you give up or keep going?
- Is there a market for the services your practice will provide?
- Who will be your potential clients?
- Will the practice have the necessary design skills and project experience to do the small but complex projects that come into such a practice?
- What skills or services will need to be bought in: IT support, accountant, bookkeeper, photographer?
- Consider the economy... is it a good time to set up? Is work available?
- Is the work available the kind of work you are interested in doing?
- How will you get the work when competing against other practices?
- Will the practice be based in a home office or rented accommodation?
- Will a home office give the right impression to your future clients?
- Where would you like the practice to be at end of years one, two and five?
- Will the practice start small and stay small, or will it start small and grow?

And here are some questions specifically for the future sole practitioner:

- Are you self-confident?
- Can you multitask?
- Will you be able to arrange cover when you are on holiday or sick?
- Are you prepared to work hard and long hours?
- Are you good with finances? You will be responsible for your money and your clients'.
- Do you have the good health, stamina and persistence that will be necessary?
- Have you got the right personality to deal with domestic clients, and can you be assertive in a positive way when dealing with difficult clients?
- Will you be able to bring in projects and maintain a balanced workload?
- Have you got the technical and project administration skills necessary?
- Can you see when you need help? Do you know how to find the right people to help?
- Do you have the support of family members?
- Will office accommodation be easy to arrange?

While you are still working for someone else, you can carry out useful preparation for your own practice:

- Get as much project administration and practice management experience as you can.
- Focus on CPD – attend business courses or do a business degree.
- Develop a network of contacts across the construction industry.
- Read books on setting up a business or an architectural practice.
- Check out government websites, articles online and in the architectural press about setting up a new business.
- Talk to architect colleagues who have already set up similar practices, visit their offices and check out their websites.
- Talk to a few non-architect colleagues who have small practices – such as a quantity surveyor or a structural engineer.
- Talk to an accountant and a bookkeeper – ideally who already work for other small practices. Find out what services they can provide.

If you are thinking of setting up on your own straight out of college, because you have been made redundant or you cannot find work, or because someone has offered you an interesting project, you will not have the luxury of earning and learning while you go through the initial stages of setting up. It will be challenging, and you will need advice from a good accountant and possibly a solicitor, a good business plan and sufficient capital, as well as the right personality – and, if possible, a good mentor.

AN ARCHITECTURAL PRACTICE IS LIKE A MARRIAGE. IT'S EASY TO RUSH INTO, BUT DIFFICULT AND EXPENSIVE TO WIND UP. TAKE IT SLOWLY, THINK THROUGH THE RISKS INVOLVED AND BE SURE IT'S WHAT YOU WANT TO DO BEFORE YOU GO ANY FURTHER.

▷ STAGE 2: Decisions

At the end of this stage you should be ready to prepare a preliminary business plan for your practice, with decisions made on the following points:

- Whether to set up as a sole practitioner, or with others.
- How to operate the practice in accordance with the ARB Architects Code: Standards of Conduct and Practice.
- The objectives of the practice.
- The type of work the practice will do and how it will bring this work in.
- The income the practice expects in the first year.
- The amount of capital available.
- The capital the practice will need in year one.
- The amount of capital the practice will borrow.
- Practice location – home office or rented office.
- The number of staff the practice will employ.
- How the practice will compete for work against competitors.
- Business training needs.
- CPD needs.
- Compliance with construction, employment and health and safety legislation.
- Expertise that will be bought in: accountant, bookkeeper, IT support, website design, etc.
- The necessary technical skills and experience for the expected work.
- The consultants and contractors the practice will recommend to clients.
- The long-term plan for the practice, for the end of years one, two and five.

The long-term plan is important, because the type of work will largely dictate the type of practice you set up. If you want to grow the practice to work on large commercial projects, then the office premises, the IT set-up and the clients will all be different from the start, compared to the practice that wants to stay small, to work mostly with domestic clients and on relatively small projects.

▷ STAGE 3: Setting up

At the end of this stage you should have decided on the type of premises you will operate from, discussed your preliminary business plan with an accountant, confirmed what capital will be available, selected a bookkeeper, decided on a company structure, obtained quotes from a specialist insurance broker and decided on a bank. You should have a clear image in your head of how the practice will operate, but you can still be working for someone else and building up more capital.

Have a meeting with your selected accountant and discuss:

- the services they can provide
- possible start dates for the new practice
- the company year/end of year accounts
- the type of company and the registration procedure
- the number of directors (for limited companies)
- the number of people the practice will employ
- the books for year one (possible appointment of a bookkeeper)
- tax and National Insurance for year one
- VAT for year one
- pension arrangements for year one
- the name for the new practice.

Select an insurance broker, and obtain quotes for:

- professional indemnity insurance
- public liability insurance
- employers' liability insurance
- building and contents insurance.

You will also need to select:

- a bookkeeper, and agree what services they will provide
- a company secretary (no longer mandatory for limited companies)
- an IT specialist if in-house skills are not available
- a solicitor (in case legal advice is needed)
- a bank for a company bank account – check their business rates.

Prepare a more developed business plan, covering the following:

- description of the architectural practice
- work – the type of work and the value range
- people (CVs)
- services provided by others (accountant, bookkeeper, IT specialist, etc.)
- office premises (home office or rented office)
- list of equipment and furniture to purchase (hardware, software, etc.)
- type of company: sole trader, partnership, limited company, etc.
- income/expenditure for year one (guesswork at this stage!)
- cashflow forecast/profit and loss forecast for year one.

Now that you know the risks and what is involved in setting up your practice, ask yourself again: Is this really what I want to do? Do I have what it takes to make this business successful? Am I ready now for the final preparation stage and to start spending money?

Once you have answered 'yes' to these questions, you are almost ready to start trading.

▷ STAGE 4: Ready to trade

On completion of this stage you will be running your own practice.

- Appoint your accountant and bookkeeper.
- Fix a date for the practice to start trading.
- If you are still working elsewhere, hand in your notice.
- Send out a notice to all your contacts, telling them about the new practice.
- If you are setting up as a limited company, decide on the number of directors and whether the company will have a company secretary.
- Instruct the accountant to set up the company and register the company with Companies House and HM Revenue and Customs (HMRC).
- Note when VAT registration is required.
- Arrange for insurance cover from the company start date.
- Confirm arrangements for office accommodation.
- Make arrangements for any staff you will be employing.
- Get the office up and running while all the paperwork goes through.
- Set up the books for year one.
- Produce a cashflow forecast/profit and loss forecast for year one.
- Set up a company bank account.
- Design the office stationery and maybe a company logo.
- Design or commission a company website.
- Set up social media accounts.
- Set up telephone and broadband accounts and a mobile phone account.
- Buy furniture and light fittings.
- Buy stationery.
- Buy or lease hardware and software.
- Produce an office manual, with copies of all standard documents.
- Produce an address book.
- Open an office diary.
- Start trading and bringing in work!

In the early days of your company, advice from your accountant is a good investment. If the company is well set up in the first place and you have a clear understanding of how it will be run and managed and the performance monitored throughout the year, there is a much better chance not only that you will be successful, but that you will be more relaxed and able to concentrate on the architectural services you aim to provide.

Succession planning, retirement, emergency plan and insolvency

It might be hard to think about closing the practice when you are setting it up, but it is important to consider and plan for the day the practice will cease trading. The office manual should have a section covering future plans for the practice, succession and planned closure of the practice, as well as an emergency plan to cover illness, accidents or the death of key individuals.

Succession planning

When founding directors or partners retire, larger practices are often passed on to a next generation of architects who may already be partners or directors of the company. Some practices are purchased by another practice. Small and very small practices, including sole practitioners, usually cease trading when the principal architect retires. This can be because your own name is attached to the practice and you do not want others to trade using your name, or because clients only come to the practice because of what you personally can offer – so think carefully about the name when setting up the practice. If you are thinking of selling your business there are specialist advisers who can assess your company and its assets and give you advice on what it is worth and how to find a purchaser. Whether you are selling or closing the practice, you will need to set up a plan – ideally at least three years in advance.

Emergency plan

Serious illness or the death of key individuals might mean the practice cannot continue to trade. To cope with such events an emergency plan should be in place and kept updated as necessary.

In a limited company where there is more than one director, the remaining directors may be able to take over and appoint a new director so the practice can continue to trade, subject to professional qualifications, or the remaining directors can arrange to close the practice.

If you are a sole practitioner, the emergency plan will be specific to your practice and your circumstances. You could ask the company accountant to be an executor of your Will, as this is a service that many accountants provide. It is important for all sole practitioners to write a Will and instruct the executors on how to close the practice and who will inherit the company assets, and a copy of the emergency plan should be kept with your Will. Any monies in a limited company bank account should be distributed to the beneficiaries, and all invoices should be paid before the company is struck off at Companies House, as once a company is struck off any remaining funds will go to the state.

If you are a sole practitioner or the sole director of a limited company you must ensure that, in the event of sudden death, arrangements are in place to hand over the work in progress, close the practice and arrange for the limited company to cease trading. Having a company secretary is no longer mandatory for limited companies, but in these circumstances it is helpful to have a company secretary who is familiar with your business and your clients, and has access to the company bank account. The company secretary does not have to be someone who works for the practice full-time. It could be the company bookkeeper, or a family member.

For sole practitioners and sole traders, your sudden death and the resulting closure of your practice would be dealt with by your executors in accordance with the instructions in your Will and your emergency plan.

All practices should keep sufficient funds in the company bank account to cover the cost of closing the practice in an emergency. These costs include professional fees (lawyer, accountant, bookkeeper and possibly a consultant architect) and PI insurance run-off costs that must be paid for a minimum of six years, even after death.

Retirement or planned closure

In the case of a pre-planned closure, for example due to the retirement of a key individual or sole practitioner, work will decrease gradually as new projects no longer come into the office. A date can be set as the last day you or anyone in the practice will give advice. PI insurance must be maintained by the company or the sole trader for a minimum of six years (or up to 12 if contracts are under seal), and this period must run from the date of the last piece of advice given. Take advice on run-off insurance from your insurance broker a year or so before you plan to retire.

Remember that while the practice is winding down the overheads will remain the same and you will still be working, but income will reduce, so financial provision should be made for this and funds set aside in the company bank account.

When the practice is going to close because a sole practitioner is retiring, a three-year wind-down programme should be produced, with a date for the company to cease trading and the insurance run-off period. During this period careful consideration must be given to what projects are accepted into the practice and how long they will take to complete, including making good defects periods. When taking on new projects during this period you should inform your clients that the practice will cease trading on a given date.

If the practice has employees who will be made redundant, they must be given notice and may be entitled to statutory or contractual redundancy.

Insolvency – failure of the business

Despite all your efforts and hard work, and all the money you have put into your business, there is still a possibility that it will fail, and these circumstances may be outside of your control. With a limited company, as soon as your liabilities are greater than your assets your company is insolvent, and it is an offence to continue to trade if your company is insolvent.

If you have a limited liability company you may be able to enter into a voluntary winding up. If you are a sole trader you may end up declaring yourself bankrupt, and you could lose your personal assets. If you are a partnership all partners could be declared bankrupt.

Always monitor cashflow carefully, and at the first sign of a cashflow problem seek professional help. The first phone call will be to your accountant. With good advice you may be able to take corrective action and save the business as well as your reputation.

The market

It is important to establish that there is a market for the product or service you are going to provide, and that you will be able to compete with your competitors. Where you chose to locate your office, the geographical area that you will cover and the range of projects you will take on will depend to a large extent on what work there is, how good you are at getting it, and the competition. The decisions you make about the new practice and the market research to support it will go hand in hand.

Key decisions

- Decide on your preferred range of projects and their value.
- Decide whether the practice will specialise in a particular field.
- Decide on the preferred client type: commercial, domestic, developers, local authority, Housing Association, healthcare, government, etc. It is unlikely that you will get commissions for public work until you have established a reputation, a trading background and a turnover history.
- Decide on the type of practice, the number of employees and the skills the practice will need to operate successfully in the preferred market.
- Decide on the geographical area the practice will cover. Will the practice have a broad project base and work locally, or a narrow project base and be prepared to cover a wider area?
- Decide on the location of the office.

Research

- Establish whether the work you want is available.
- Obtain information about possible future building programmes or funding for regeneration projects in the area.
- Establish who your competitors are and how they are getting work.
- Look at competitors' websites, the staff numbers they employ and their client base.
- Speak to individuals who commission buildings and find out what they look for in an architectural practice.
- Speak to developers who do design and build and employ architects.
- Establish how to pitch for the available work if there is an established process.
- Establish a fee structure that will make your practice competitive but profitable.
- Speak to other architects who run similar practices and do similar work.
- Speak to consultants and contractors who are already working in the field.
- Establish the criteria for getting on to local authority or Housing Association shortlists.
- Attend local meetings, join local organisations, read journals, look at local authority websites, follow relevant blogs and Twitter accounts. Attend RIBA regional or branch meetings.

Once you have done the research and know the market, and you have decided what type and size of practice you want and where it should be located, you can develop a business plan.

Regardless of the area you choose to work in, and for even the smallest domestic projects, you should develop a good relationship with each client and maintain this throughout the project and beyond.

REMEMBER THAT A SUCCESSFUL SMALL PROJECT WITH A SATISFIED CLIENT COULD LEAD TO A LARGER COMMISSION FROM THE SAME CLIENT, OR A REFERRAL TO ANOTHER CLIENT.

Alternative company structures

The very small architectural practice will normally be a sole trader or a limited liability company. Partnerships and limited liability partnerships are less common these days. Your accountant or lawyer will be able to advise you on which option is best for your circumstances, and once you have decided which best fits your requirements you should be able to find all the current information you need either on the government website or the Companies House website. It is possible to change the name or the structure of your business after a few years of trading, but making a well-informed choice when setting up should avoid the need to do this.

Sole trader

It is easy to set up as a sole trader and, despite the term, you can take on employees. As a sole trader your tax status is 'self-employed' and you will pay Income Tax on the profits of the company. The tax status of employees will be PAYE (pay as you earn). However, you are totally responsible for the debts of the company and if you cannot pay them you may have to declare yourself bankrupt and risk losing your possessions or even your home.

Limited liability company

Many small architectural practices are set up as limited liability companies. The limited liability company structure works equally well for a sole practitioner as for larger practices. Having a limited liability company can give your business more credibility than if you operate as a sole trader. It allows the practice to grow and directors to join and leave the practice, but the biggest single advantage is that the limited company is responsible for what it does and personal assets are not linked to the company. However, if you are a company director and you have a bank loan, the bank manager may ask you for a personal guarantee. Also, individual liability can remain in tort. Overdraft facilities may also require a director's personal guarantee.

If you set up a limited company, your business stationery must show the following information:

- the registered name of your company
- all (or none) of the names of the directors
- the place of registration
- the registered company address
- the company registration number.

Partnership

The type of company structure you will adopt is one of the most important decisions you will make when setting up a new practice, so make sure that you obtain advice and that you have carefully considered all the advantages, disadvantages and risks before making a decision.

> LEGAL ADVICE SHOULD BE SOUGHT FOR PARTNERSHIP
> OR LIMITED LIABILITY PARTNERSHIP COMPANY
> STRUCTURES.

COMPANY STRUCTURE	ADVANTAGES	DISADVANTAGES	TAX AND NATIONAL INSURANCE
Sole trader	Easy to set up Less onerous accounting	Liability is unlimited Personal assets are not separate from business assets	Register for NI with HMRC Pay Class 2 NI contributions Pay Class 4 NI contributions Self-employed status for sole trader PAYE applies (for any employees) Income Tax payable on profit Company may have to register for VAT
Private limited liability company	Separate legal identity Easy to set up Greater credibility Easier to raise finance Easier to remove a director than a partner Directors can join and leave the company Limited liability Can be set up by one person Can have a company secretary* Lower tax Possible to defer tax by retaining money in the company Directors' pension contributions are tax efficient** Personal assets are separate from business assets Dividends can be paid NI can be reduced by paying in dividends Entitlement to more state benefits than as a sole trader	Detailed accounts required by law Accounts must be filed at Companies House and are available to the public online Named person with significant control (PSC) Name and address available to the public online Annual confirmation statement (previously annual return) is obligatory Penalty for late filing of accounts Less flexibility for dealing with company losses Individual liability can remain in tort***	Companies Act 2006 applies Register with Companies House before trading Register for NI with HMRC Class 1 NI contributions paid by employer and employee PAYE applies to directors and employees Corporation Tax payable on profit Dividends can be paid to directors Company may have to register for VAT
Partnership	Similar to sole trader Get solicitor's advice on partnership agreement	Similar to sole trader Partners are jointly liable	Self-employed tax and NI status for partners PAYE for employees
Limited liability partnership	Similar to limited liability company Get solicitor's advice on partnership agreement	Similar to limited liability company Partners are not jointly liable	Self-employed tax and NI status for partners PAYE for employees

*Although no longer mandatory it is beneficial for sole practitioners/sole directors of limited liability companies to appoint a company secretary. This means that in the case of an emergency, such as the death of the sole director, there is someone with knowledge of the company and with access to the company bank account.

**Tax changes from year to year so always check current tax information online.

***Tort is a civil responsibility for causing injury or loss to another party, as opposed to a responsibility laid out in a contract.

Architects Registration Board (ARB)

The Architects Registration Board is the body set up by Parliament as the independent UK regulator of architects. Anyone who is involved in designing and constructing buildings, and describes themselves as an architect, must be registered with the ARB.

Architects Code: Standards of Conduct and Practice

As an architect you are expected to:

- be honest and act with integrity
- be competent
- promote your services honestly and responsibly
- manage your business competently
- consider the wider impact of your work
- carry out your work faithfully and conscientiously
- be trustworthy and look after your clients' money properly
- have appropriate insurance arrangements
- maintain the reputation of architects
- deal with disputes or complaints appropriately
- cooperate with regulatory requirements and investigations
- have respect for others.

The Architects Code: Standards of Conduct and Practice can be found on the ARB website.[3]

Royal Institute of British Architects (RIBA)

The Royal Institute of British Architects is a professional body for architects, primarily in the United Kingdom but also internationally, founded for the advancement of architecture under its charter. Membership of the RIBA has many advantages but is not mandatory for architects.

The RIBA values

Honesty, integrity and competency, as well as concern for others and for the environment, are the foundations of the RIBA's three principles of professional conduct, set out below. All members of the RIBA are required to comply.

THE THREE PRINCIPLES

1. **Integrity:** Members shall act with integrity and honesty at all times.
2. **Competence:** In the performance of their work Members shall act competently, conscientiously and responsibly. Members must be able to provide the knowledge, the ability and the financial and technical resources appropriate for their work.
3. **Relationships:** Members shall respect the relevant rights and interests of others.

The supporting Guidance Notes include the following sections:

1. Integrity, Conflicts of Interest, Confidentiality and Privacy, Corruption and Bribery.
2. Competition.
3. Advertising.
4. Appointments.
5. Insurance.
6. CPD.
7. Relationships.
8. Employment and Equal Opportunities.
9. Complaints and Dispute Resolution.

The Code of Conduct and the supporting Guidance Notes can be found on the RIBA website, www.architecture.com.[4]

RIBA accreditation: Chartered Practice, Conservation Architect

RIBA Chartered Practice accreditation

Once you have set up your new company you must decide whether the practice is to be an RIBA Chartered Practice. Small practices and even sole practitioners can apply for RIBA Chartered Practice accreditation at any stage. This could be after the first year, once the practice is more established.

SOLE PRACTITIONERS MAY BE CHARTERED ARCHITECTS EVEN IF THEIR PRACTICES ARE NOT CHARTERED PRACTICES.

The main advantages of practice accreditation are:

- RIBA assurance of a quality service for your clients
- good management systems
- employment support
- marketing promotion – only chartered practices will be promoted by the RIBA
- listing in the RIBA chartered practice directory
- use of the RIBA chartered practice insignia on your letterhead and signboards
- access to business support services.

In order to register your practice you must complete an application, pay a yearly subscription and comply with certain criteria relating to CPD, health and safety, employment policy, PI insurance cover and quality management systems. Directors or partners must be RIBA Chartered Architects and members of the ARB, and you will be asked to participate in benchmarking surveys.

Full details and application forms are available from the RIBA.

RIBA Conservation Architect Accreditation

Both the RIBA and the SPAB (Society for the Protection of Ancient Buildings) run courses for architects who wish to specialise in conservation work or the refurbishment of old buildings. Individual architects who already have some experience and are willing to comply with the International Council on Monuments and Sites (ICOMOS) Guidelines on Conservation can apply for RIBA accreditation at various levels:

- **CR:** Conservation Registrant – capable, basic knowledge and skills, some experience
- **CA:** Conservation Architect – skilled and experienced
- **SCA:** Specialist Conservation Architect – expert

In order to register for conservation accreditation you must already have some experience, and you must complete an application with case studies and pay a yearly subscription. Accreditation is valid for five years. Full details and application forms are available from the RIBA.

THE ADVANTAGE OF ACCREDITATION IS THAT YOU ARE MORE LIKELY TO GET WORK IN THIS SECTOR ESPECIALLY IF YOU WANT TO WORK ON GRADE I – OR GRADE II – LISTED BUILDINGS.

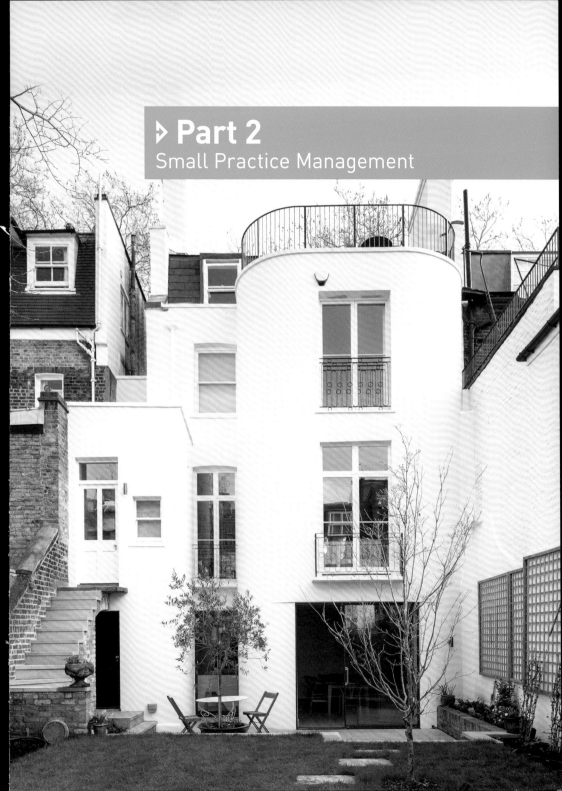

FINANCIAL MANAGEMENT

Business plan, cashflow forecast, profit and loss forecast

Business plan

The RIBA Business Benchmarking Survey 2012/13 showed that 62% of architectural practices did not have a business plan, and that only 13% planned beyond the current year.[5] This might explain why some architectural practices do not make much money, even if they work hard and produce good buildings.

No matter how small the practice, even if you are a sole practitioner, every practice should have a business strategy and a plan for the coming year and the longer-term future. When putting together a business plan bear in mind that you will use this document if you have to borrow capital at any point, whether in the first year of the practice or in subsequent years. The first business plan will include some guesswork about income and may make reference to relevant experience gained elsewhere, but from the second year onward the plan will reference targets that have been met, completed projects and actual turnover.

Ask your accountant or an experienced colleague to have a look at your draft business plan and give their opinion before you speak to the bank if you are hoping to borrow money.

To decide what information is relevant to the business plan, ask yourself what a bank or a relative investing in your company would want to know about you, your finances and your new company, then write this down. For the small practice or a sole practitioner, a small amount of text and a few spreadsheets (based on your last set of company accounts) that can be read and digested in 10–15 minutes should be sufficient.

It's always hard to find time in a busy small practice, and you will be juggling priorities daily. Keep the format simple so it is quick and easy to update at least once a year. A good time to do this is after you have checked and signed the company accounts. Don't let day-to-day deadlines on projects distract you from the longer-term objectives of the practice.

Be realistic with targets for income and growth so that in future years you will be able to demonstrate that you have met them.

A small practice might have a four- to six-page business plan, including the following sections:

- A one-page practice description:
  - name(s) of director(s)
  - skills and experience; any specialist expertise
  - type of work
  - client base
  - how work is sourced
  - office location
  - consultants employed by the practice
  - approach to it, social media, website, etc.
  - other relevant activities undertaken by the practice.
- CV(s) of director(s).
- A list of completed contracts, with the value and a short description.
- Work on listed buildings or in conservation areas.
- Turnover and profit for the past five years.
- Workload programme for the coming year.
- A long-term programme.
- Cashflow forecast and profit and loss forecast for the coming year.
- A balance sheet.

Mark the business plan 'confidential', and arrange the signature of a simple non-disclosure agreement if you leave it with a third party such as the bank.

Cashflow forecast and profit and loss forecast

One of the advantages of having a limited company is that the accounts must be prepared in considerable detail, usually by an accountant, and an abbreviated account will be submitted to Companies House at the end of the company year. This account can provide all the information necessary to prepare a cashflow forecast for the coming year. If the practice is small and intends to stay small, and the previous year's net profit was in line with the target set, it should not take longer than a few hours to produce a new cashflow forecast and profit and loss forecast.

> **FORECASTS ARE ESSENTIAL TO THE SUCCESS OF YOUR BUSINESS. FAILURE TO FORECAST ACCURATELY AND MONITOR TARGETS COULD LEAD TO CASHFLOW PROBLEMS, LIQUIDATION OF YOUR COMPANY OR BANKRUPTCY IF YOU ARE A SOLE TRADER.**

As the year progresses you should make periodic checks that income is meeting the target set, and take action if income is falling short. If income cannot be increased, see whether the admin and overhead costs can be reduced. If income is not on target you may not be able to pay out planned dividends or make a one-off pension contribution as planned.

Monthly cashflow forecast

The purpose of the cashflow forecast is to ensure that there will always be enough cash in the company bank account throughout the year to make all payments when they are due.

- The 'company year' will start on the date you decide for your company.
- The 'financial year' is the same for everyone, and starts on 6 April every year.

CASHFLOW FORECAST

MONTHS (company year)	1	2	3	4	5	6	7	8	9	10	11	12
Bank balance at start of month												
INCOME												
Capital												
Income (fees)												
VAT income												
EXPENDITURE												
Rent												
Salaries and dividends												
Tax: PAYE, NI and Corporation Tax												
VAT to HMRC												
Council Tax or business rates												
Bank charges												
Loan interest												
Pension(s)												
Insurance												
Energy bills												
Phone bills												
Licences for software												
Travel												
Other expenses: • stationery • printing • postage • hardware and software • training/cpd • professional subs • consultants • cleaner.												
Bank balance at end of month												

All the figures you put in the table opposite will be estimates in year one, and you may have to do quite a lot of guesswork, but after year one you will be able to use the previous year's figures as a reference and be more accurate. You should be able to say where the figures come from if asked.

To update the cashflow forecast, record your outgoings under the same headings used in the original cashflow forecast.

The most important figure is the income to date from fees, and this can easily be checked on an ongoing basis. For example, if the target fee income for a sole practitioner is £80k/year the target for each month will be £6.66k and the quarterly target will be £20k. A quick check against fees invoiced to date and paid will show whether the income targets are being met. Monthly expenditure can be controlled in the same way using the monthly expenses sheets and a bank statement.

Regular invoicing and prompt payment are important so you can check that your income is on target. If you do work in January you should aim to get paid in January as soon as the work or stage is complete and an invoice has been issued. Make the terms of payment clear in your appointment contract as well as the rate of interest on late payments.

You should have an overdraft facility in place with the company bank in case of the need for short-term cashflow, but it is wise to have a reasonable cash reserve in the company bank account or another reserve of capital so one or two late payments or some unexpected expenditure will not force you to rely on the overdraft facility.

Monthly profit and loss forecast

The purpose of a profit and loss forecast is to see how profitable your business is. VAT is not listed, as this is simply a tax that you collect and forward to the government.

PROFIT AND LOSS FORECAST

MONTHS (company year)	1	2	3	4	5	6	7	8	9	10	11	12
INCOME												
Capital												
Income (fees)												
Other income												
GROSS PROFIT												
LESS EXPENDITURE												
Rent												
Salaries and dividends												
Tax: PAYE, NI Corporation Tax												
VAT to HMRC												
Council Tax or business rates												
Bank charges												
Loan interest												
Pension(s)												
Insurance												
Energy bills												
Phone bills												
Licences for software												
Travel												
Other expenses: • printing • postage • hardware and software • training/cpd • professional subs • consultants • cleaner.												
NET PROFIT												

If you exceed your target income this will enable you to set more ambitious targets for the coming year. Some practices will have one cashflow forecast to show the bank, and another more ambitious one for internal use. However, in a very small practice or when working as a sole practitioner your time is probably better spent on projects that are bringing in income.

Remember to set aside enough cash for the large lump sum payment you might have to make to pay Corporation Tax on the net profit of the company in the previous financial year. If your accountant submits your accounts at the last minute you might not get much notice of when the tax payment is due.

If you are hoping to raise capital you may be asked to provide your previous cashflow forecasts and profit and loss forecasts, so keep these records simple and accurate. If necessary, ask your accountant to prepare this information and discuss it with you before you approach the bank.

If income is less than expected, maybe there is time and scope to reduce the overheads to compensate and reduce the risk of going into your overdraft. Remember that regular outgoings will not go down even if the fee income does, and when you borrow money it must be paid back with interest.

Clients will sometimes run company checks on their architects (if they are limited companies), so it is best not to operate with a bank balance tottering close to the red line – this might give the impression that the practice is too small to do the project, or at risk of going under.

Raising money, making a profit and the company bank account

Raising money

You will need to have a business plan and a cashflow forecast to work out how much money you need to borrow, how long you need it for, who you can approach and what security you can offer.

Do not underestimate how difficult it will be to raise capital, and when you ask for a loan make sure it is for the right amount as it may not be possible to ask for more money later.

A good rule of thumb is not to use up all your own money before trying to raise more money. Your investor will want you to invest in your business as well to be sure you are committed, so will not be impressed if you say all your own money has already been spent.

There are a few different ways to raise money depending on whether you are doing this alone or with others:

- loan from the company director(s)
- loan from a family member or friend
- bank overdraft for short-term borrowing
- bank loan for longer-term borrowing
- selling shares in the business
- taking a partner (seek legal advice before entering into a partnership)
- second mortgage on your house.

There are pros and cons with all of the above, and potential risks such as being asked to provide personal guarantees or high rates of interest, so make sure you have made the right decision for your business and prepare your presentation carefully with input from your accountant as necessary.

Making a profit

Along with every other small business, the challenge you face is that everything is constantly changing and moving. If you run out of money, your business will fail. You cannot afford to not monitor your financial affairs. The first step for a business is to break even, and then to be considered successful you must make a profit.

Profit is important, as it will give you the opportunity to expand the business in whatever way you choose and will provide a healthy balance in your bank account that will not only make the company more credible, but will also help to balance the books if future months prove more difficult than expected or the odd invoice is paid late.

Controlling cash in an architectural practice means careful monthly monitoring of your debtors and creditors, and the company bank account. The better this control is, the more likely you are to see any warning signs early enough to take action. For a small practice the amount of paperwork relating to expenditure is relatively small, and the number of invoices coming in and going out will be limited, so it is easy to keep a summary sheet of income to date in any financial year. It is important to invoice regularly and to keep on top of the paperwork and chase payment if necessary. Sometimes this will mean prioritising the chasing of an invoice over another task or deadline in the office. For the small practice this constant prioritising of tasks is an essential skill that you will use daily.

If you are working as a sole practitioner you will know and deal with everything yourself, but if you employ staff and delegate parts of the business it is important to have weekly/monthly meetings to review performance and targets, and to agree and take whatever action is necessary.

You can run out of cash for a number of reasons:

- You might not be doing enough work.
- You might not be spending enough time on productive (fee earning) work.
- Your fees might be too low.
- Your invoices might not be going out promptly.
- Your invoices might not have been paid promptly or in full, or at all.
- Your overheads, including salaries, are too high relative to the income of the practice.

The company bank account

There is no reason why you should use the same bank for your business account as for your personal account. Before setting up a new company bank account decide what advice, services and facilities you need, including overdraft and loan facilities. Check what services the different banks will provide as well as their charges, and whether there is any advantage to using a bank that has a local branch with an approachable manager you can meet when you need advice.

Charges and services vary from bank to bank for business accounts, so it is worth doing some research and shopping around.

If you have a loan from the bank, check what information the bank will need from you and how frequently.

If interest rates increase it might be worth having more than one account so cash can be moved from a current account to a savings account. However, when interest rates are low, there is little merit in doing this.

Accounts and bookkeeping

When you set up your practice you must decide what company structure to adopt and what kind of accounts you will need. It is best to take professional advice on this. It is not necessary to understand all the different types of accounting systems, but it is crucial that you understand the accounting system selected for your particular business. Regardless of who prepares the accounts, remember that you will sign them and be responsible for them.

A sole practitioner/sole trader with a small turnover might opt to do their own bookkeeping and do simple cash accounting with minimal input from an accountant at the end of the year, but unless you are short of architectural work and good with figures it makes much more sense to employ your skills as an architect to do architectural work, as this will maximise your income, and you can then employ a bookkeeper and an accountant to do the books and the accounts, run your PAYE system and do the VAT returns.

 CHOOSE YOUR ACCOUNTANT AND BOOKKEEPER CAREFULLY. TRY TO FIND PEOPLE WHO UNDERSTAND THE SCALE AND NEEDS OF YOUR PARTICULAR BUSINESS, WHOM YOU CAN RELY ON TO MEET DEADLINES, AND WITH WHOM YOU WILL ENJOY WORKING — POTENTIALLY FOR A LONG TIME.

Remember that your accountant and your bookkeeper are not just the providers of spreadsheets, information and accounts required by HMRC, HM Customs & Excise (HMC&E) or Companies House. They are your colleagues, who care about what they do and what they bring to your business. If you work remotely try to make a point of meeting up with them at least once a year.

Because many small architectural practices are set up as limited companies, the advice in this section focuses on the bookkeeping and the company accounts that limited companies must prepare and submit to Companies House each year. The same systems could serve a sole trader equally well, although sole traders have the option to use simple cash accounting if their businesses are very small.

If you engage the services of a bookkeeper and an accountant you will have little to do other than provide information on a quarterly basis to your bookkeeper, and check and sign the company accounts when issued by your accountant at the end of each company year.

Accountant services

The services provided by your accountant can include the following:

- Preparation of your full annual accounts.
- Preparation of your abbreviated accounts for Companies House (limited companies only).
- Corporation tax calculation and advice on deadline for payment.
- Preparation and return of P11D (listing your benefits/expenses in the year) to HMRC.
- Preparation and return of P35/P14 (deductions from employees' salaries reconciled to payments to HMRC).
- General advice during the year, including advice on employment legislation, how to run your company in a tax-efficient way with regard to payment by salary or dividends, and pension contributions.
- (Optional) Preparation and online submission of the company director's personal tax return.

Some years your accountant will do nothing more than prepare the end-of-year accounts, submit various forms to the tax office and calculate the Corporation Tax liability, but it is helpful to know that you can discuss various matters and get advice from your accountant during the year as well.

Bookkeeping services

The services provided by your bookkeeper can include the following:

- Making quarterly VAT returns and payment to HMC&E.
- Running the PAYE system and sending information to HMRC.
- Issuing P60 to employees (shows total salary in the tax year and PAYE and National Insurance deductions).
- Advising you on take-home pay, tax and National Insurance monthly payments.
- Providing accountant with quarterly and yearly summary spreadsheets so the end-of-year accounts can be prepared.

Your bookkeeper will be able to run your PAYE system and set up the spreadsheets to be used throughout the year to record income and expenditure, so that the company accounts can be prepared by your accountant at the end of each company year.

The bookkeeping spreadsheets will include:

- **INCOME** – invoice payments, bank interest.
- **EXPENDITURE** – salaries, tax, petty cash, bank charges, purchase day book items.
- **PURCHASE DAY BOOK** – goods and services purchased: payments to consultants, Companies House, furniture, software, etc.
- **SALES DAY BOOK** – list of invoices with separate columns for % fee, time charge fees and expenses.
- **PETTY CASH** – separate columns for stationery, postage, printing, travel, etc.
- **VAT CONTROL** – amounts paid to HMC&E.

In order for your bookkeeper to have all the information necessary to prepare the above spreadsheets and to do the VAT returns each quarter, you must provide the following information on a quarterly basis just before the VAT return is due:

- Bank statements (showing BACS payments in, direct debit payments, purchases and any interest).
- Invoices to the practice.
- Expenses sheets relating to the quarter (petty cash).
- Mileage sheets relating to the quarter.
- Copies of dividends.
- Telephone bills.
- Cheques issued and received (very rare now).
- Correspondence from HMRC, HMC&E, Companies House, etc.
- Gift Aid payments.

In a small office you should be able to keep all the above information in one filing tray, so at the end of each quarter the paperwork for the bookkeeper is ready and in one place. It should not take longer than an hour for you to sort the paperwork into bundles and hand it over to the bookkeeper. Your bookkeeper may not even need to come to the office, as the information can be sent by email or post. This paperwork should also be properly archived, as you might need it in the event of a tax office investigation.

Tax and invoices

Tax

As a small architectural practice and limited liability company the various taxes that will apply are as follows:

PAYE
HMRC will provide a tax code for each individual employed by your company, including directors, and tax on salary payments will be deducted at source. Employer's contribution is also paid monthly.

NATIONAL INSURANCE
National insurance (NI) is paid monthly to HMRC.

CORPORATION TAX

Corporation Tax is paid once a year to HMRC and is based on the company net profit shown in the company accounts. Remember to set aside enough cash to pay this tax. (Sole traders will pay Income Tax rather than Corporation Tax on the profits of their company).

VAT

As a business you collect this tax from your clients and pass it on quarterly to HMC&E. You must register for VAT if the turnover of your company exceeds £83k (this value may change) in any 12-month period, and once registered you must charge your clients VAT on all the services you provide. If your business falls below the threshold you can de-register. As a business registered for VAT you will be able to claim back any VAT your company pays on purchases or services.

There are various ways of dealing with VAT depending on the size and turnover of your business:

- Registered for VAT (you charge VAT and you claim back VAT paid – quarterly).
- Registered for the VAT flat-rate scheme (you pay a flat % – yearly).
- Not registered if your turnover is sufficiently low.

The tax office will notify you of the dates when returns and payments are due. Late returns or late payments will result in a fine or interest being charged.

CAPITAL GAINS TAX

You may be liable for tax on any profit if you sell your business assets, including property, furniture or equipment.

Making a loss

If the company has a bad year and makes a loss it may be possible to offset this against tax due on profit in other years. Your accountant will advise you how best to deal with this loss, and the tax regulations applicable at the time of the loss.

Personal Income Tax

For company directors it makes sense for the practice accountant to do your personal tax returns as well. They will already have all the details about your employment income. All you need to do is provide details of any private pension contributions and any income not related to your company, such as interest on savings accounts or dividends on shares or rental income. Your accountant will also be able to tell you how much you must pay, and when.

Directors who take part of their income in the form of dividends will be paying tax monthly through PAYE and topping up with lump sums twice a year (31 January and 31 July). These lump sums are based on the assumption that your income in the coming year will be the same as in the previous year. On receipt of your tax return the tax office will notify you how much you must pay, or how much is to be refunded, and the deadlines.

Tax investigation

Remember that it is illegal to conceal any earnings from the tax office, and you should try to avoid any investigation by the tax authorities. You can do this by ensuring that all income is declared, your accounts are sufficiently up to date and accurate, and that your returns are filed and payments are made on time. Having an agent to do this for you will help.

Tax invoices

Tax invoices that are sent to your clients should include the following details:

- invoice number
- name, address and registration number of your company and where the company was registered, and the name of all or some of the directors
- name and address of your client
- date of the invoice
- date of the service
- description of the goods or services
- company VAT registration number (if the company is registered for VAT)
- total amount invoiced
- VAT rate
- bank details (sort code and account number).

Copies of your invoices should be archived. Each invoice amount should be recorded on a spreadsheet so that income to date can be calculated at any point during the year in seconds.

Overheads

It is important for the long-term success of your business to establish the right balance between income and expenditure. Fee income in any architectural practice will vary from year to year, but most of your overheads (rent, salaries, software licences, etc.) will remain fixed.

The typical overheads for a small architectural practice include:

- rent (unless you work from a home office)
- business rates (unless you work from a home office)
- staff costs, including salaries, pension contributions, NI
- furniture
- equipment
- hardware
- software and licences
- insurance
- bank charges
- consultants' fees
- cleaning and maintenance
- heating and lighting bills
- phone bills
- tax
- travel and mileage
- petty cash:
  - postage
  - stationery
  - documents (OS maps, Joint Contracts Tribunal (JCT) or RIBA contracts, RIBA appointment documents, etc.).

Some of this will be capital expenditure, such as furniture or computers that will last for more than two years. These items will depreciate over time and the depreciation will be accounted for in your end-of-year accounts.

The other items are revenue expenditure, and these items are allowable as expenses that can be deducted from your gross profit to calculate the net profit on which your company Corporation Tax will be based.

Any petty cash expenditure during each month should be recorded on an expenses sheet, with copies of all receipts stapled to the sheet. At the end of each month you will be paid back for any mileage or out-of-pocket expenses on behalf of the company. These expenses sheets should be archived.

> IF YOUR PRACTICE IS BASED IN A HOME OFFICE YOU WILL BE ABLE TO CHARGE YOUR PRACTICE FOR PART OF THE COST OF RUNNING YOUR HOME (HEATING, LIGHTING, MAINTENANCE, INSURANCE, ETC.). YOUR ACCOUNTANT WILL ADVISE ON THE AMOUNT THAT IS REASONABLE TO CHARGE TO THE PRACTICE.

Fees

The way you charge for your services will depend on the size and type of work. The fee can be a combination of the following methods of charging:

- time charges
- percentage fees
- lump sum fees.

Percentage fees

For domestic work, a percentage fee based on the construction cost is the traditional way of charging for architectural services. The percentage is based on the initial budget for construction, but at the end of the project the percentage is based on the final account figure – you should explain to your clients how this works. The benefit of this fee structure is that it is self-adjusting throughout the project, so as your client adds work to the project and the construction cost increases the fee increases without the need for further negotiation. You will need to keep your client informed of any increase in the construction cost and the overall cost of the project, and obtain their agreement to the revised cost.

The RIBA used to issue a fee graph showing the recommended percentage fee appropriate to every type of project for both new-build and refurbishment work, but this graph and the idea of mandatory fees were scrapped in favour of the free market. However, there is nothing to stop you having your own in-house fee graph similar to the old RIBA one to help you set percentage fees. As long as the fee has been carefully set at the right level, the method works well.

The percentage fee covers the basic services from the RIBA Plan of Work Stages 2–6. Services at Stage 1 and additional services during Stages 2–6 can be charged on an hourly basis. The percentage and any hourly charged services should be explained to your client and confirmed in the appointment contract before you start work. You can also show fees on the Plan of Work. Any change to the appointment contract (such as the construction cost on which your fee is based) should be agreed with the client and confirmed in writing.

The total percentage fee can be broken down into the RIBA Plan of Work Stages as follows:

RIBA PLAN OF WORK STAGE		CUMULATIVE FEE
0	STRATEGIC DEFINITION	Time charge (£/hour x estimate of hours)
1	PREPARATION AND BRIEF	Time Charge (£/hour x estimate of hours)
2	CONCEPT DESIGN	15%
3	DEVELOPED DESIGN	35%
4	TECHNICAL DESIGN	70%
5	CONSTRUCTION	100%
6	HANDOVER AND CLOSE OUT	Included above
7	IN USE	Time charge (estimate in hours)

RIBA Fee Calculator

The RIBA provides guidance on how to calculate fees using the RIBA Fee Calculator.[6] With this guidance and the RIBA Plan of Work 2013 you will be able to give a detailed breakdown of the service you will provide at each stage, the fees at each stage and the total fee. If you agree a total fee at appointment you will also have to agree the basis on which you will be paid for any additional work, and how this will be measured. Domestic clients almost always add in work at every stage of the project or take work out and substitute it with other work, so you must ensure in advance that you will be paid for any extra or abortive work.

Lump sum fee

If your client asks you to agree a lump sum fee, explain that the fee will be based on a fixed scope of work. Explain that any work not included in the original brief will be charged for separately on an hourly basis. This explanation is often enough to persuade a domestic client that a percentage fee is probably a better option, as most of these clients add work to the contract at every stage.

Time charge

Other services that are not included in your percentage fee can be charged on a time basis, such as feasibility studies at Stage 1, or additional submissions to planning, or negotiating a contract instead of going out to tender.

On very small projects (£40,000 and less) it may be appropriate to charge on a time basis rather than a percentage fee. Your total fee can be based on an estimate of the time the project will take and broken down into Stages 1–6. If your estimate will be exceeded you must agree in advance the additional time necessary. For example, if you estimate that six site visits are necessary to administer the contract but eight site visits are required, you must agree the additional cost of the two site visits in advance. If your client adds work into the contract you must also estimate and agree the additional time required.

Expenses

Expenses will be incurred on all your projects (travel, parking, printing, postage, purchase of contracts, OS maps, etc.) so you should make it clear in your appointment that these expenses will be counter-charged to the client and will be in addition to your percentage fee or time charge fees.

Working for nothing

In the early days of our practice a psychiatrist friend made a wise observation: 'If you work for free you will always have work!'

Not all the work you take on will be as productive as intended or make the profit you had in mind, but you should never agree to provide professional services for free, as you will always be liable for professional advice given. If you charge properly you are more likely to have your time and your work appreciated. Further guidance on this topic is included in Part 3, under 'The Architect's Appointment'.

Competitions

If your practice enters competitions for which there is no guaranteed payment or fee, you must ensure that sufficient funds are available within the practice to cover this, and that the lack of payment for this work will be offset by other profitable projects in the practice. A competition can benefit the practice in other ways: it might raise the profile of the practice, generate a project that will look good on the practice website or allow you to gain experience in a new area of work. If you win the competition you might secure the project (and the future of the practice), so it could prove a good investment of time. Sadly not all projects for new buildings won through competition are built.

Chasing money and reducing the risk of bad debt

There are various ways of reducing the risk of bad debt within your practice.

- Make it clear in your appointment document what fees you will charge and when, and your terms. Make sure that your client has read and understood all the terms and signed the appointment contract before you do any work or issue any information.

- At the end of each work stage agree with your client that all information has been provided and that they are happy for you to submit an invoice before you proceed to the next stage. Clients who are warned that an invoice is on its way and have agreed to it in principle will usually pay promptly.

- Invoice at regular intervals on all the projects in the office so that each invoice is a reasonable amount relative to the scale of the work and your client can remember what work the invoice relates to.

- If an invoice is not paid within the agreed number of days, speak to your client and issue a reminder.

- If a client queries your invoice in writing:

  - Ask your client to be specific about the query and to withhold only an appropriate amount from the total on the invoice.

  - If your client's query is reasonable, admit it and deal with the issue then ask your client to confirm they are satisfied.

  - If the query is not reasonable, set up a meeting and put the project on hold until the matter is resolved. No client will want their project to be on hold, so there is an incentive to resolve the query quickly.

- If you proceed to the next stage prior to payment of the invoice for the previous stage, do not issue the new information until the last invoice is paid.

- Despite what they have agreed in your appointment contract some clients will be slow or reluctant to pay your fees, so you will need to chase them and charge any additional costs in accordance with your agreed terms.

  - As soon as the invoice is overdue politely write to your client asking for the money.

  - Seven days later politely write again.

  - Seven days later phone to ask for an explanation and try to get a promise that they will pay.

- Keep the pressure up.
- Remind your client that late payment will trigger interest charges at the rate agreed.
- If you are paid by cheque, cash it immediately to make sure it does not bounce.
- For persistent non-payment send a formal letter warning that the next step is to take legal action or to use a debt collection agency.
- Tell the client that you are considering using the Small Claims Court or County Court (your client will not want a County Court Judgment against them as this could affect their credit rating).
- As a last resort you may terminate your contract prior to completion of the project.

Very occasionally a client will find fault with your work to justify withholding payment. They may wait until receipt of court papers before paying, or worse, on receipt of court papers they may make a counter-claim that will mean you must involve your insurers. Immediately you have a situation that could cost you far more than the outstanding fee. If you can spot the type of person who will behave like this early enough, try to avoid working with them in the first place. Not only will they waste a lot of your time, they will be unpleasant to work with and could cost you a lot of money. If you are halfway through a project before the client reveals their true colours, accept the fact that they will be difficult and decide how you will deal with the situation. Seek advice if necessary and invoice on a regular basis for small amounts.

Good financial management is important, especially when it comes to the collection of money that is owed to the business.

MANY GOOD ARCHITECTS WORK HARD AND DESIGN GREAT BUILDINGS BUT GO OUT OF BUSINESS BECAUSE OF POOR FINANCIAL MANAGEMENT.

OFFICE MANAGEMENT

Practice objectives

The objectives will vary, but every practice should have objectives and these should be recorded in the business plan. The objectives should be agreed by all parties and reviewed regularly. It is all too easy to accept an interesting project that can quite suddenly take the practice in a different direction to the one originally intended, or sooner than intended.

The sudden offer of a project with a big budget and a good fee might be tempting, especially if you have the technical skill and experience to produce the contract documents. However, before deciding to accept the commission you must decide whether it is the right job for your practice now, whether you want the practice to grow that quickly, and how the project will affect staff numbers, office accommodation, PI, furniture, hardware and software, and your cashflow. You will also have to consider whether this is a one-off project and if other projects of a similar size are likely in the future.

Many practices will want to make a good profit and grow the practice as quickly as possible, but not all practices will have these as their prime objectives. A sole practitioner architect might put a stronger emphasis on work/life balance than profit or growth, and their objectives could be as follows:

- To run the practice from a home office.
- To work alone or with one other architect.
- To bring in enough work to make the practice viable as a business.
- To bring in work as required and to avoid peaks and troughs in workload.
- To work on projects of particular interest to the practice, for example, domestic refurbishment.
- To limit the value of projects accepted into the practice (upper and lower limits).
- To work with preferred clients, contractors and consultants.
- To establish a sound client base so that new work is sourced by word of mouth.
- To establish a portfolio of built work to bring in new work through the website.
- To have the work of the practice widely published.

Whatever your practice objectives, they should be reviewed at least once a year when the business plan is updated, as the objectives will evolve and shift over time. Always have an eye on the future and know where you want the practice to be in one, two and five years' – time and make these objectives realistic so you don't feel you have failed if your target is not achieved.

Where will your office be located?

Your office will say a lot about you and the practice, and the cost of premises will vary significantly. There are a number of options, ranging from the use of a room in your house to building your own office premises. The home office might be suitable for one or two people, but not if the practice is three or four strong already and hoping to grow.

After salaries the cost of premises is likely to be the most significant outgoing, so the cost and the type of premises must be carefully considered before you make a decision, and this should be reviewed each year.

If the small practice is to be successful all aspects of the business must be carefully weighed up. If the office accommodation is too expensive, it will make the overheads high and could reduce salaries or put pressure on the office to take on work that pays more but is less interesting, or make staff members feel they must work around the clock to balance the books. If the office accommodation is cramped or dated, not easily accessible or in the wrong location then it could put clients off as well as demoralising the staff.

The home office

If you are setting up as a sole practitioner or employing only one person, you intend to maintain a small practice by choice, your main area of work is going to be domestic, and you have space in your house, a home office can be ideal. You will lose the use of a spare room but the reduced overheads will give your practice a huge advantage over the competitors in rented accommodation, as you will be able to allocate more resources to projects and still make a profit.

Thanks to technological advances it is now possible to run a successful small architectural practice from a relatively small space, such as a single room in your own house or a purpose-built room at the end of the garden, as long as family members are in agreement and the accommodation complies with health and safety legislation. If you are planning to employ staff you may require planning permission for a change of use. Be careful that you do not become liable for business rates and later on Capital Gains Tax if you sell your house when it has been used for business purposes. Your accountant will be able to advise you on this.

The big advantage of a home office is the significant cost saving on rent and cleaning, and bills and business rates. The cost of travel is also eliminated, and the travelling time and energy that is saved can be put to good use doing something else such as a walk or a swim before starting work. You can also make lunch in your own kitchen. You will be in for tradespeople or delivery of packages (which might mean you take in packages for everyone on your street!).

You will need suitable building and contents' insurance; not all domestic policies cover the use of the home for business so check with your insurance broker and change your insurance provider if necessary.

If the practice is taking on residential work, the clients who come to the home office will see the rest of the house so it needs to be safe, clean and accessible by car or public transport. If your house is well presented it can be one of the best advertisements for the work you do.

Despite all the advantages of a home office, young architects might find that working from home is lonely and reduces the opportunities for networking and learning from others. Younger architects may have young families and the house might be too chaotic or noisy a place to work and hold meetings with clients. For noisy homes the room at the end of the garden might still be an option, as office activities can then be completely separate from home activities.

Leasing premises

Your office will say a lot about your business, so you will want to choose a space that you can afford, is pleasant to visit, will make the right impression on your clients and will be a nice place to work and to relax with colleagues during breaks. A building beside a canal or river, or a nice view from a meeting room window, or a small sunny terrace with some plants can make even a small space feel more relaxed and interesting.

Availability and the cost of accommodation will vary enormously between areas. The location, the cost of the rent and all associated costs, the length of the lease and any restrictions all need to be carefully considered before you make a decision. Remember, these overheads will not reduce even if the office has little or no work.

There are significant differences between working from a home office and committing to a lease.

Factors to consider when selecting office premises

- Length and terms of the lease, including: insurance, repair and maintenance, any restrictions or break clauses, the cost of the rent and any deposit.
- Other costs such as business rates and energy bills.
- Availability of building floor plans.
- Space ready to use or fit-out required – and at what cost?
- Cost of furniture, hardware and software.
- Size and type of practice.
- Is more space available if the practice grows? Can space be reduced if the practice shrinks?
- Accommodation needed: reception, meeting space, studio space, admin space, filing/library/archive space, storage, WC and shower, food and drinks preparation area.
- Does the practice need a street presence or can it be located on the top floor?
- Impression given by location and building.

- Other building occupants.
- Accessibility for employees and clients; wheelchair access.
- Public transport, car and bike parking.
- Security (for the premises and your staff).
- Fire safety and means of escape; fire alarm.
- Security alarm.
- Good lighting and ventilation (natural and mechanical).
- Adequacy of heating, lighting, power and data.
- Noise from the outside.
- Can all the windows be opened for natural ventilation?
- Access to services (sandwich shops, printers, etc.)
- Cleaning, running and maintenance costs.
- Compliance with health and safety and employment legislation.[7]

Items covered by the Workplace (Health, Safety and Welfare) Regulations 1992 include the temperature of the office, lighting levels, ventilation, space standards, sanitary facilities, water for drinking and an area for eating.

You should ask your solicitor to check any business lease to make sure it is suitable for your business. The landlord may request proof of the practice's ability to pay the rent, a set of audited accounts and a deposit. You may also be required to return the property in the same condition as you found it, so you must budget for decoration and any repairs at the end of the lease.

Serviced accommodation

Some small practices opt for serviced accommodation in a good location like Central London. This can be expensive but has the advantage of being more flexible, with shorter rental periods, while also giving clients the impression of a well set-up office in a convenient central location with shared meeting room or reception facilities and access to printers. If shared by other architects or consultants these premises might also be a more stimulating environment for young architects, and may provide opportunities for collaboration and networking with other architects and consultants, or sharing CPD events.

Buy or build your own office

If you have sufficient capital and you are prepared to tie it up, you could consider buying your own property or building a new one. This could be a small or medium-sized building, and it might also provide opportunities for subletting, depending on the size of the premises and your own practice. The practice will pay rent and this will partly offset the loan repayments or capital invested.

However, buildings are not always a good investment and it is a lot of capital to tie up for a long time, so seek professional advice as to whether this is a good option under your circumstances. Another option might be to build your own premises then sell and lease back the same property.

Managing the premises

Running costs will include:

- gas, electricity and water
- cleaning
- insurance
- security
- maintenance and repair
- service contracts for security or other equipment
- waste collection
- service charges (if applicable).

The responsibility for these tasks should be allocated to one employee or to an office manager if the office is large enough to employ one.

Equipment, hardware, software and BIM

When setting up a new practice you will need a comfortable and quiet space as an office, in an accessible location and with WC, and don't forget tea-making facilities. It should be large enough to hold meetings, but you do not need much furniture, equipment or hardware. In fact, with digital technology, online communication and cloud storage, you probably already have most of what you need on a laptop. You must comply with the Health and Safety at Work Regulations even if you are working in a home office or at the end of the garden.

Furniture

Each workstation will need a desk, some layout space and a comfortable office chair, and you will need a table at which you can have meetings with your clients or with contractors, as well as some shelves and cupboard storage for books, stationery and archives. Archive storage should be off the premises, or in a separate room with a fire door, so it is more likely to survive in case of a fire in the office.

Hardware

- workstation(s) with one or two monitors per station
- laptop(s) – not essential
- telephone – landline(s) and/or mobile(s)
- printer/scanner/copier (A3 and A4).

You will also need reliable, fast and uninterrupted internet access and a range of useful sundries: back-up hard drives, cameras, measuring tapes, torches, screwdrivers, manhole keys, and so on.

Software

This will vary depending on whether the office uses PCs or Macs, as well as in-house software preferences and staff drawing skills. It is an advantage if your computer-aided design (CAD) software is compatible with the software used by other consultants you will work with, including the structural engineer, quantity surveyor and the company that provides you with surveys of existing buildings.

The list of software below would be sufficient for a sole practitioner or a very small office.

PURPOSE	SOFTWARE
CAD drawings	AutoCAD or AutoCAD LT
BIM (not every small practice will use BIM)	Revit or Revit LT
Presentations	Microsoft PowerPoint
Spreadsheets	Microsoft Excel
Specifications	NBS Minor Works, NBS Intermediate
Word-processing	Microsoft Word
3D	SketchUp, AutoCAD, Revit
Virus protection	Various providers
Sending photos	Dropbox or similar
Working with PDFs	Adobe Acrobat or Reader

Software licences

Some software and updates can be purchased outright, but most CAD and NBS specification software is now leased on a yearly contract, and updates are included in the lease. The advantage of a lease is that you do not have the same initial capital cost as when purchasing the software and it is always up to date, but the lease arrangements are expensive and when the lease expires you own nothing. You need to assess carefully what software the practice needs and limit the cost of numerous leases. Some leasing companies also provide IT support.

BIM

BIM (Building Information Modelling) is not yet widely used by small practices for small and domestic projects, but this is changing as BIM becomes more widely used on large projects and architects become more familiar with the software, the associated terminology and the advantages.

THE COST OF BIM SOFTWARE AND STAFF TRAINING IS STILL A SIGNIFICANT OVERHEAD FOR A SMALL PRACTICE, SO THIS NEEDS TO BE CAREFULLY CONSIDERED ALONG WITH ANY ADVANTAGES.

BIM can be provided at three different levels. For small and domestic projects Level 1 is appropriate, where the architect is the BIM manager and owner of the BIM model. The BIM execution plan prepared by the architect will describe (using a spreadsheet) how information modelling will be managed and carried out during the project, and what information will be issued at each stage, and will also incorporate the employer's information requirements.

Information can be issued to consultants who do not have BIM software in 2D, and 2D information provided by the consultants can be added to the 3D model by the architect. Information for the domestic client produced with BIM software can be issued in PDF format.

The benefits of using Level 1 BIM include the obvious appeal and uses of a 3D model, and automatic coordination of the model with schedules. Revisions to the model are also added automatically to schedules, and cost estimates can be produced from the model. Level 2 BIM compliance (which means that all parties exchange information between their BIM models) is now compulsory on all public sector construction projects.

When deciding whether or not to invest in BIM, you need to decide:

- Whether your clients have any need or use of a BIM model.
- What level of BIM is appropriate to your practice.
- What hardware and software is best suited to the level of BIM at which you will operate.
- Whether the BIM software selected will upgrade to Level 2 or 3.
- What the cost of setting up a BIM workstation is, and how many you need.
- What the cost of leasing BIM software will be on a yearly basis.
- What in-house skills are required, and the cost of training.
- Whether BIM can be provided for the same fees, or if fees must increase.
- What advantages BIM can bring to the practice.
- Whether BIM will be used on selected projects or all projects.
- Who will carry out surveys of existing buildings, and the cost of surveys.
- Note that BIM Level 2 has been set as the minimum method of working on all public sector projects since April 2016.

Before deciding to use BIM, try to speak to a BIM manager in another practice of a similar size to yours and that does similar work, and establish what software they use, what their BIM protocol is for small projects, and whether the decision to use BIM has increased turnover or profit, or the growth and success of the practice.

The RIBA bookshop has a good selection of books on all levels of BIM, including BIM for small practices.

The office manual/quality control

The first step to developing a quality control procedure is to compile an office manual that sets down the principles of running the practice. The quality management systems should be appropriate to the size of the practice. The manual can contain ARB and RIBA codes of conduct; marketing, staff and admin information; financial information; information relating to design and contract administration; and standard documents. The manual should be set up in the early days of the practice when workload is light, and then updated as systems and procedures in the office are refined and developed. Putting a manual together and keeping it up to date will take time, but it will ensure a consistent approach to the employment of staff, the running of projects and the admin tasks in the office. New employees will be taken through the manual during their induction training and subsequently they will be able to use the manual to find, produce and save information in line with office policy and without needing to ask too many questions.

If you are a sole practitioner, you should be able to put all the information relating to your practice in one file. If you have employees, some sections of the manual could be only for use by the director(s), sole trader or partners, with other sections for employees. Keep the manual simple, with only the information you need to run the practice, as the more information there is the more time it will take to update it. Ideally make one person responsible for keeping the manual up to date, and allocate sufficient time for this task.

The contents of the office manual can include some or all of the following sections, depending on the office filing and administration systems and whether you employ staff and have an office manager, or work as a sole practitioner.

General

- ARB Architects Code: Standards of Conduct and Practice.
- RIBA Code of Professional Conduct.
- Relevant legislation, Building Regulations and British Standards.

Office

- office premises information
- inventory of office furniture and fittings
- list of equipment and hardware
- address book
- insurance policies
- quality control procedures
- a copy of the current year business plan
- cover/succession plan/retirement plan/emergency plan
- RIBA Chartered Practice information (for Chartered Practices)
- RIBA Conservation Architect information (for accredited architects)
- practice objectives
- current workload/programme
- website and social media details
- practice brochure
- project types and value range
- promotion of the practice and sourcing work
- client complaints procedure
- list of software and licences, virus protection and IT support
- RIBA appointment contracts or standard letter contracts used by the practice
- preliminary site consultation form
- correspondence and filing
- information and knowledge management (paper and digital)
- backup of digital information (drawings, documents, email, photos)
- archive storage
- diary events.

Tax and finance

- fees
- invoices
- accountant duties
- bookkeeper duties
- tax
- salaries and dividends
- Companies House information (for limited companies)
- banking details.

Staff

- practice employment policy
- practice health and safety policy (office and site visits)
- terms of employment
- salaries
- holidays, sickness and cover arrangements
- office hours
- CVs
- accreditation details
- pension arrangements
- procedure for reviews, complaints, discipline, confidentiality
- induction, training and CPD
- resource allocation and performance analysis.

Project administration

- list of RIBA and JCT construction contracts used by the practice
- RIBA Plan of Work – traditional procurement
- CDM Regulations 2015 – duties
- preliminary site consultation with client – agenda
- pre-contract meeting – agenda
- pre-contract programme
- brief and changes to brief
- cost control
- permissions and approvals
- correspondence
- collection, sharing and filing of project information
- CAD drawing protocol
- BIM
- information on drawings
- NBS specification
- tender process
- contractor selection and contractor appointment
- feedback (Plan of Work Stages 1–6)
- project archive list.

Office stationery

A separate file with copies of all office stationery can be useful.
The contents might include:

- letterhead
- invoice
- compliments slip
- business card
- time sheet
- expenses sheet
- mileage sheet
- phone sheet
- print sheet
- postage sheet
- job contact sheet
- fee income summary sheet
- dividend payments summary sheet
- snagging/defects inspection sheet
- title block for A4 and A3 drawings
- drawing issue register
- CPD/training sheet
- archive box label
- office workload programme
- pre-contract programme
- workload programme
- site instruction
- interim certificate, Practical Completion certificate, making good defects certificate, non-completion certificate
- sample spreadsheet – pricing document/tender analysis/valuations/final account.

Information management, library, backup and archiving

Office address book

Even sole practitioners and very small architectural practices will have hundreds of names and contact details for past and current clients, consultants, contractors, subcontractors, tradespeople, planning departments, building inspectors, specialist suppliers, the tax office, the bank, and so on. It is important to store this information in such a way that you can find, not just a telephone number, but also the name of the person or company you need.

Outlook and Google are invaluable when searching for information, but if you want to remember the name of a subcontractor who worked on a certain job ten years ago, or even the name of a client, the office address book is still useful. The address book can be a digital file kept on your desktop, or it might be hard copy. You should be able to find the information you need quickly, perhaps even while you are on the phone to a client.

The address book might include the following sections:

- project contact sheets filed in job number order
- job number and client list for each year
- consultants
- contractors
- specialist subcontractors
- tradespeople.

Office library

Most up-to-date technical information can be accessed online, obviating the need for anything other than a small library in the office for architectural books and books relating to the business side of the practice.

Apart from technical information on products, other key documents can also be accessed online – such as the Building Regulations, the Party Wall Act, and the ARB and RIBA codes of conduct. Government websites provide information about company structures, legislation, tax, and so on.

British Standards

The British Standards can be purchased online, but they are expensive. It is possible to buy a contract for access to all the British Standards online, but these contracts are also expensive for small practices that might not use the service frequently and only require a limited number. The cost of the standards referred to in the NBS Minor Works Specification for even a small job could run to thousands of pounds, so you need to consider carefully which ones you or the contractor on site will need, and have copies of these standards in the office. If you refer to a British Standard that you have purchased on a previous contract, make sure by checking online that it is still current.

Document reference system

Some of the information and records in the office will be filed in paper format, but increasingly information is stored digitally. From day one you will need to set up a standard office model for allocating job numbers and saving documents. The model should be used consistently for all the documents produced in the office by all members of staff.

It is important that everybody in the office uses the same system for naming and storing documents. Remember that people move on, but the information they produce needs to remain accessible to others – perhaps for years after the documents are produced.

The reference for each document must be on the hard copy of the document to enable the digital copy to be found easily.

Drawing protocol

For all drawings produced in the office, a drawing protocol should be established so that they are produced in exactly the same way, and when printed they look consistent. Title blocks on the drawings should also be based on a standard.

BIM protocol

BIM Level 1 is appropriate for small and domestic projects. When using BIM, the client's requirements should be agreed at Stage 1. The BIM execution plan (BEP) will clarify in the form of a spreadsheet who is responsible for the BIM model, and the information that will be exchanged at each stage of the project.

Backing up

There are various ways of backing up digital information, and this should be done on a regular basis. When deciding how often to back up, consider what the cost wuuld be to your practice if all the information between backups were lost.

You can back up to the cloud or a separate drive that should be stored away from the office. Remember that your backup should include all your photos and emails, as well as all project files and admin files.

Archiving

Good archiving of job files and other office admin documents, such as the practice insurance policies, bills and invoices, correspondence from the tax office and so on, is essential and will require dedicated storage space in the office or off site.

A good archive will have all the information you might ever need, but no more than this. The full archive for each project should be kept for a minimum of six years after completion of the contract (12 years if contracts are under seal). The RIBA recommends that key documents should be kept for 17 to 20 years.

Archive checklist for a domestic project:

- job number
- address
- date of practical completion
- contact list (client, contractor and consultants)
- architect's signed appointment, including any revisions
- planning permission or certificate of lawful development
- listed building consent (if applicable)
- Building Regulations plans approval
- Building Regulations completion certificate
- JCT or RIBA contract (or a copy if the client has kept the original)
- electrical certificate
- boiler installation certificate
- gas safety certificate
- damp and timber survey, report and guarantee
- flat roof guarantee
- glass guarantee
- door and window guarantees
- asbestos – demolition and refurbishment survey and report
- invoices for asbestos removal (if applicable)
- accepted tender
- tender analysis
- contractor and client insurance details
- certificates
- final account
- site instructions
- tender document and construction information
- as-built drawings
- party wall agreements
- progress photos
- health and safety file contents list.

It may also be prudent to keep minutes of meetings, handwritten notes or drawings from site meetings, and correspondence with the client for at least six years. Some of the above information can be stored digitally, including the progress photos, as long as there is a digital backup somewhere else.

In addition, the office should have copies (or access to copies) of all email correspondence. If a claim is made against the practice, this email correspondence can provide much of the detail and dates necessary to defend the claim.

Project filing

Each project in the office will have a few associated files with information under appropriate headings. Depending on the size of the project, there might be separate files for pre-construction and construction. Files can be digital or hard copy.

Headings for a domestic project might include:

- client
- structural engineer
- services engineer
- quantity surveyor
- party wall surveyor
- planning
- building control
- contractor
- subcontractors
- suppliers
- technical information
- site instructions
- valuations and certificates
- minutes of meetings
- site notes
- drawing issue sheets
- survey
- tender.

A separate hard copy or digital file might contain Stage 1 and 2 drawings, Stage 3 planning drawings, Stage 4 tender drawings and Stage 5 construction issue drawings, specifications and schedules.

Having the information you need on site

If the practice has numerous small jobs on site at different stages and you are doing weekly site visits, it is reassuring as well as time-efficient to have a system that means you always have the necessary information to hand. A system that works well in our office is to have a clear plastic filing box for each project on one shelf in the office. This file is taken on site visits and contains the tender document incorporating the NBS specification, A3 tender drawings, construction drawings issued during construction, and a full set of site instructions to date. As revised A3 drawings are issued, they are stapled to the original tender drawings. This way, the project architect has a copy of all the relevant information on site, including what was priced at tender stage. Any verbal instructions or sketches made on site are kept in the file until a formal site instruction is issued.

The important thing is to have a system that enables quick access to information. All the above could be on a tablet or even a phone, but remember that a small digital screen is sometimes difficult to see on site if it is sunny, or if you are explaining something to more than one person.

On domestic projects where the client is likely to make many changes during construction resulting in revised drawings, always check on site that the contractor and the subcontractors are working to the latest issue.

The role of the practice manager

A sole practitioner is by default the practice manager as well. If the office is small, perhaps the duties of the practice manager are also carried out by an architect, or shared between architects. A larger office will probably employ a dedicated office manager.

The practice manager's duties and responsibilities might include:

- day-to-day running of the practice
- general administration
- office premises
- utilities (gas, water, electricity)
- phones and broadband
- insurance
- equipment
- supplies
- stationery
- health and safety
- security
- fire – means of escape
- software updates
- software licences
- recruitment
- training/CPD
- reviews
- information management
- quality control
- communication
- backup
- archive
- office manual updates
- business plan updates
- petty cash
- fee invoices
- chasing payment
- passing VAT paperwork to the bookkeeper or accountant.

PI and other insurance

The main insurance policies for a small architectural practice are:

- Professional indemnity insurance (mandatory).
- Employers' liability insurance (mandatory).
- Public liability insurance (recommended).
- Building and contents' insurance.
- Car insurance (if you use your personal car for business travel you must include this business use on your policy).

Apart from the insurance policies you are required to hold by law, there are many other types of insurance you might have, including travel, private healthcare, permanent healthcare, personal accident, data loss or identity fraud, and so on. Decide what cover your practice needs and take professional advice to ensure your practice has the appropriate level of cover.

The RIBA can recommend insurance brokers who will provide advice and quotes for insurance that complies with the ARB requirements for minimum cover. The cost of insurance can vary, so it might be worth shopping around.

Professional indemnity (PI) insurance

PI insurance can be obtained from specialist brokers, and each year before renewal you must fill out detailed forms relating to your practice income and the level of cover required. Make sure you complete the forms accurately, as failure to declare something important could invalidate your policy. Architects who do basement work might need to accept an increased excess on these projects due to an increased number of claims relating to basements in recent years, so again it is worth shopping around to find the right cover for your practice.

Bear in mind that, if you stay with the same insurance broker from year to year, you will establish a good working relationship, and you will benefit from the advice they can provide if you are concerned about a potential claim. However, it is your insurers or their lawyers, rather than your brokers, who will deal with any actual claim.

Copies of your insurance policies for each year going back to the first year of the practice should be kept in a safe, accessible place in the office in case a claim is made against the practice. Some clients will ask you to provide evidence of your PI cover, and your insurance broker will be able to provide a certificate.

Public sector clients may ask for a very high level of PI cover, which might preclude your practice from bidding for public sector projects unless you are prepared to increase your cover and keep the higher cover in future years. It may be acceptable to confirm that cover will be taken out if the job is won.

Always read the policy that your insurance broker recommends before proceeding. Check for compliance with ARB requirements, limits to the cover, that cover is available for each and every claim, that legal costs are covered, and any exemptions.

The ARB issues guidelines on cover. The minimum is currently £250,000 for each and every claim. However, many small practices, even sole practitioners, will need higher levels of insurance cover than £250,000. The premiums will vary from year to year and will be based on the value of projects completed in previous years, the type of work, and any claims made.

PI run-off cover

When your company stops trading, you are required to provide run-off cover for a minimum of six years (12 years if you have signed or administered contracts under seal). Your broker may advise you to hold cover for longer than the minimum period.

The level of PI cover during the run-off period will probably be based on the highest level of cover held in the previous three years. You must hold insurance at the time a claim is made. It is not enough to have been insured at the time of the incident.

Notification

You must notify your insurers of the circumstances as soon as you are aware that a claim may be made, otherwise your insurance cover may be invalidated. You should also be careful to provide all relevant information when completing application forms. If you fail to do so, you may invalidate your insurance.

Current and further information about mandatory professional indemnity insurance cover for architects can be found on the ARB website.[8]

Building and contents' insurance

You will need to insure the office premises and the contents. This means that, in the event of a fire or flood, you will be able to get the practice back up and running as soon as possible.

If you are running a business from a home office, you must check that your current policy covers the use of your home as an office. If not, change your policy provider to ensure that your business is covered. Check, too, that your insurance will cover employees' personal possessions.

Make an inventory of all the furniture, equipment, computers and stored material in the office, and keep a copy in the office manual, which should be updated regularly. Check that your policy will replace old with new in the event of a claim. Any items you take out of the office, such as laptops or tablets, should be listed on the policy.

Make sure you are aware of any online risks, for which your practice may need additional cover with a separate policy. Such risks include viruses, fraud, hacking, theft and so on. Your IT consultant will be able to provide advice on how your systems should be set up to minimise the risks, and may warn you of other risks.

Employers' liability insurance

To comply with the Employers' Liability (Compulsory Insurance) Act 1969, employers must hold insurance cover of minimum £5,000,000 and must display a certificate in a prominent position in the office. This insurance covers employees' illnesses or injuries caused on or off site. There are exemptions, such as for companies employing only their owner, so check with your insurance broker before taking out this insurance.

Public liability insurance

This insurance cover is recommended, but not mandatory. It will cover third parties when they visit your practice, or damage to the property of third parties caused by the practice employees when they visit other premises or sites.

Health and safety policy

Health and safety law applies to employees working in the office, and when they are on building sites or other premises. The main legislation is the Health and Safety at Work Act 1974. Other acts and more recent regulations relating to health and safety are listed on page 201.

Every practice should base its health and safety policy on a risk assessment, and a copy of the policy should be filed in the office manual. The RIBA publishes a template for adoption online, and RIBA Chartered Practices must set out their policy in writing and apply it to all employees. New employees should be given a copy of the office policy as part of their induction.

The main elements of the policy for a small architectural practice will be:

- Health and safety risk assessment.
- Duties of the practice manager relating to health and safety.
- Fire – protection from fire and means of escape from the office.
- CDM Regulations 2015 – duties.
- In the office:
  - use of VDU screens
  - chairs and workstations
  - visitors to the office
  - hazardous substances
  - accidents
  - illness (physical and mental)
  - smoking.

- Site visits:
  - Employees must not survey a building on their own.
  - Employees must write in the office diary the time they leave the office and when they expect to return.
  - Employees must only visit a site during daylight and when the contractor is present.
  - Employees must follow site rules when on site and avoid any unsafe practice.
  - Employees must carry a mobile phone when out of the office and on site.
  - Employees must wear protective footwear and suitable clothing when on site to reduce the risk of injury.
  - Employees must report any accident or injury on site.

Employers should consider not only risks and physical illness, but the mental health of employees, such as stress caused by working conditions.

First-aid

The Health and Safety (First-Aid) Regulations 1981 apply to all employers. Requirements include:

- Having a trained first-aider on site.
- Access to a first-aid kit.

Emergencies

In the case of a serious fire and loss of all computers and files, the practice should be able to set up elsewhere on a temporary basis. It should be able to rely on backups and information stored away from the office or in the cloud to continue to run, pending reinstatement of the premises and replacement of equipment.

Diary events and year planner

Every small practice will be subject to deadlines for tax payments, returns to Companies House (for limited companies), payment of subscriptions and renewal of leases, and monthly bills paid by direct debit, as well as regular tasks such as backing up or performance reviews.

You will receive reminders from HMRC, the VAT office and from Companies House, and your accountant and your bookkeeper will request information at specified intervals. Key items and dates can be listed and flagged in the office diary. Some will be specific to your practice and your accounting dates, and other items will relate to the tax year.

It is helpful to have a simple schedule of the events and tasks with dates for action filed in the office manual. The list might include the following:

DIARY EVENTS FOR A LIMITED LIABILITY COMPANY	
ITEM	DATE
Financial year	6 April–5 April
End of your company year	Date specific to your company
PAYE tax and employer's National Insurance paid to HMRC	Monthly
P11D return (form with details of employees' expenses to HMRC)	Annually
P35 return (a summary of the deductions made from the employees' salaries reconciled to the payments made to HMRC during the tax year)	Annually
P60 – end-of-year certificate	Annually
VAT returns and payments	Quarterly
End-of-year abbreviated accounts to Companies House	Annually
Annual return to Companies House (online)	Annually
Corporation Tax	Annually
Insurance:	Annually
• PI	
• Public liability	
• Employers' liability	
• Building and contents.	

DIARY EVENTS FOR A LIMITED LIABILITY COMPANY (continued)	
ITEM	**DATE**
Other:	Annually
• subscriptions and licences	
• ARB, RIBA membership	
• software and anti-virus licences	
• domain name renewal	
• web hosting renewal	
• cloud storage renewal.	
Rent	Monthly
Business rates/Council Tax	Monthly
Telephones, mobiles and broadband	Monthly
Utilities (gas, water, electricity)	Monthly

REGULAR OFFICE TASKS	
ITEM	**DATE**
Backup	Daily
Invoicing update	Weekly
Office workload programme update	Monthly, or as necessary
Allocate resources to projects/Analyse performance against target	Monthly
Monitor fee income against targets	Quarterly
Business plan update for the practice	Annually, or as necessary
Salary reviews	Annually
Performance reviews	Annually
Update the office website/social media	Weekly

Bringing in work

Before trying to source work, you must decide what work you want to do, how profitable it will be and whether you have the skills to do it, and that the work is out there so you can pitch for it.

For example, if you have a small practice based in London, and the practice specialises in domestic refurbishments and conservation work, you should have no problem bringing in work. There are thousands of houses in London that are more than a hundred years old, most of which need work doing, and there are plenty of wealthy clients who want to refurbish, alter or extend their homes. Work is relatively easy to source if the practice has a good website and portfolio of completed projects, but this work is complex and profit margins can be tight. Not all practices can make domestic work viable, so it is important to understand the resources you will need for each project and negotiate the right fee.

Larger practices, or small practices with aspirations to grow, will have a marketing plan and a strategy for sourcing projects. This is covered in Part 1, and more detailed advice on the topic can be found in the RIBA *Handbook of Practice Management.*[9]

Word of mouth

To bring in new work by word of mouth from existing clients, make sure you invest enough time on every project so that it is well designed, well managed, accurately costed, adequately resourced and finished to a high standard, including all snagging items. After Practical Completion, make sure you deal with any urgent defects during the defects period, and sign off any other defects at the end of the defects period. Check with your clients at the end of each stage that they are happy with the design and cost information provided. This all takes time, but if done well your clients are likely to recommend your practice to their friends or family, or use the practice again themselves.

One of the biggest advantages of working from a home office is the low office overheads, so you can afford to allocate not only a senior architect but more time to each project than a practice with higher overheads operating from commercial premises.

Office brochure

As well as having a website, the practice can have a printed brochure. For a small practice, this could be as simple as a two-page document with a few carefully chosen images (one image is worth a thousand words!) and some preliminary guidance on fees – information that will not be published on your website. If the brochure is for domestic clients, it can describe in simple terms the services an architect can provide on a domestic project, and a short description of the necessary approvals. Before meeting a new client, check that the brochure information is up to date, then print a copy and give it to them at the first meeting. It is not a good idea to have hundreds of brochures printed professionally, as they may go out of date and have to be binned before you get a chance to use them. After the first meeting and an informal discussion about fees, services and budget – and once you have obtained an in-principle agreement with your client – you can then send out the (more daunting for a domestic client) RIBA appointment contract for signature.

Practice website

No matter how small your practice is, and even if you are a sole practitioner, it's worth commissioning a specialist website designer, and a professional photographer for your completed projects. You will still need to write the text and select the photographs, and comment on the proposals at each stage of development. Make sure you allocate enough time for this expensive exercise to make sure you get the best website possible and a good return on your investment.

The website should be set up in such a way that it comes up quickly in online searches, and it should be updated regularly with new photos and news targeted at your potential clients. Avoid lots of text and tiny or pale print, as some clients might not be able to read it. Most clients only require a small amount of legible text on a website, as they will tend to focus on the project photographs. They will probably then look for a phone number or email address to contact the practice directly. When taking calls, remember that the client's first phone call to you might be one of several others they are making. This first call is therefore important, as the client will be deciding whether or not they want to ask you to take on their project. On your website you can also have links to social media networks such as Facebook or Twitter.

**CHECK OUT THE WEBSITES OF YOUR COMPETITORS EVERY
NOW AND THEN, AND IMAGINE YOU ARE A POTENTIAL
CLIENT — MAKE SURE YOU ARE DOING EVERYTHING AS
WELL AS THE COMPETITION.**

A presence on other websites

If your practice does domestic work and you have good photos on your own website, you may be asked to have a presence on a website such as Houzz. com. Increasingly, this website is used by domestic clients to collect images of what they like and want. The consultants you work with may also ask you if they can give information about your practice or use photos of your jobs on their websites. Always check with the photographer that you have permission to use and publish their photos in this way.

Using social media

Used appropriately, social networks can increase awareness of your practice, enable feedback and bring in new business. The main networks of use to architects are Facebook, LinkedIn, Twitter, Pinterest and Google. However, be aware of the time required to keep on top of social media along with everything else you will be doing, especially if you are a sole practitioner. Constructive criticism can be helpful, but if you receive negative feedback this way and do not deal with it, this could actually harm your business. If you do not have time to keep up with social media, but you feel it would be good for your business, you could consider paying a company or your website designer to do it for you.

Beware of participating in friendly banter in public, as this could alienate potential clients. It is important to keep your private life separate from your professional life.

Publishing your work

Try to have your work published in the architectural press, and if you are looking for domestic work, in the magazines targeted at your potential clients. Having high-quality photos of your work taken by a professional photographer will make it much easier to have it published.

Competitions

Competitions can be a good way to get experience of designing a building type in which you have an interest. If you win a competition, the practice might get the commission for the whole project, and this could provide work and future growth opportunities for the practice. However, even with limited competitions there is never a guarantee of winning, so you may end up doing a significant amount of work for no fee. However, such work is not necessarily abortive as the project could still be used on the website to show other potential clients your experience, and in this way it might help to secure a future commission.

Awards

Winning an award may mean your work is widely published, and the award can be noted on your website. It can bring your work to the attention of potential new clients and add credibility to your practice. There are numerous yearly awards aimed at small projects, so make a list of these with the deadline dates and consider entering your recently completed projects.

Repeat clients

Repeat clients can be a great source of new work. It is much easier to work with someone you know and understand already than with a new contact. Also, they were clearly impressed with the services provided if they are coming back to your practice.

It is rare to get repeat domestic clients because few have the opportunity of carrying out more than one project on a house, but in our practice we have had a few where our clients moved to other properties. We have also done many projects for one private school – 12 projects in total over a 14-year period.

Referrals

If your practice does domestic work, colleagues you have worked with previously may refer clients to your practice. Architect colleagues may also employ your practice to carry out projects on their own homes, or recommend you to their family members or friends. Other consultants and contractors familiar with the practice may also refer work.

The more people out there who know you, the type of work you do, the quality of your work and the service you provide, the more likely you are to be recommended to potential new clients.

Existing projects

Existing projects nearly always grow, creating more work and more fees. This is a good source of new work as long as you have sufficient resources to cope, and providing you have set up your appointment to allow for appropriate fees to cover the extra work. Domestic clients will probably add work into the project at each stage, and even when the project is on site, no matter how hard you try to fix the brief at Stage 2. For this reason a percentage fee is ideal for domestic work (see pages 59–60) as it means you will not have to go back to your client to negotiate a revised fee every time they add work to the contract. However, you must keep your client informed of the estimated overall cost of the project at each stage, both pre-contract (Stages 2–4) and during construction (Stage 5).

The unexpected commission

Always keep some resources available for an emergency, or for a phone call that brings in a new and exciting project. Depending on your own specialisms and the set-up of your practice, an exciting project can mean various things:

- It could be a new house on an interesting site, or the refurbishment of a Grade II-listed building in Central London.
- It could be a project that will be lucrative for the practice.
- It could be a project that will allow the practice to grow or move office.
- It could be a job for a prestigious client that you would like to have on your list.

If you need to expand the practice, or even move office to take on a new project, make sure that this is in line with your long-term plans, and that the office can handle the disruption. Update your cashflow forecast and your profit and loss forecast, and only accept the commission when you are sure the project is right for the office.

NEVER BE TEMPTED TO TAKE ON TOO MUCH WORK RELATIVE TO THE RESOURCES YOU CAN MAKE AVAILABLE.

On top of the project work already in the office, you need time to keep on top of office administration, invoicing, chasing payment, CPD, training and the inevitable queries from site or client changes to a brief that you cannot plan for.

Workload programme

ABC ARCHITECTS
OFFICE WORKLOAD PROGRAMME
Ref: ....
Date..............................

		2017																						
JOB No	**ADDRESS**	January					February				March				April				May					June		
	Week commencing Monday	2	9	16	23	30	6	13	20	27	6	13	20	27	3	10	17	24	1	8	15	22	29	5	12	19
1609	Address A					6MD																				
1610	Address B	CONSTRUCTION																								
1701	Address 1	PRE CONTRACT													TENDER/LEAD IN				CONSTRUCTION							
1702	Address 2							PRE CONTRACT														TENDER/LEAD				
1703	Address 3														PRE CONTRACT											
1704	Address 4																									
1705	Address 5																									
etc																										
	Unconfirmed jobs																									
1706	Address																									
1707	Address																									

You cannot rely on your memory alone when you run a small practice that does lots of jobs. There will be hundreds of things to remember, and things rarely happen when they are supposed to. Even if you carefully plan ahead each day and week, things can change at short notice.

There are various ways to keep on top of all that is happening in the practice, but workload programmes are an important part of this. The real value of such a programme is the relative ease and speed with which it can be updated, and how much information can be shown on one page.

You will need an office workload programme showing every job in the office, whether at pre-construction stage or on site, as well as including the jobs that are in the defects liability period and those for which your appointment has not yet been confirmed. The programme should be updated at least once a month, as there will be slippage on some contracts, new ones will be confirmed and some may have fallen through or fallen further behind. Colour coding can be helpful, with everything on site shown as red, pre-contract work yellow, approval

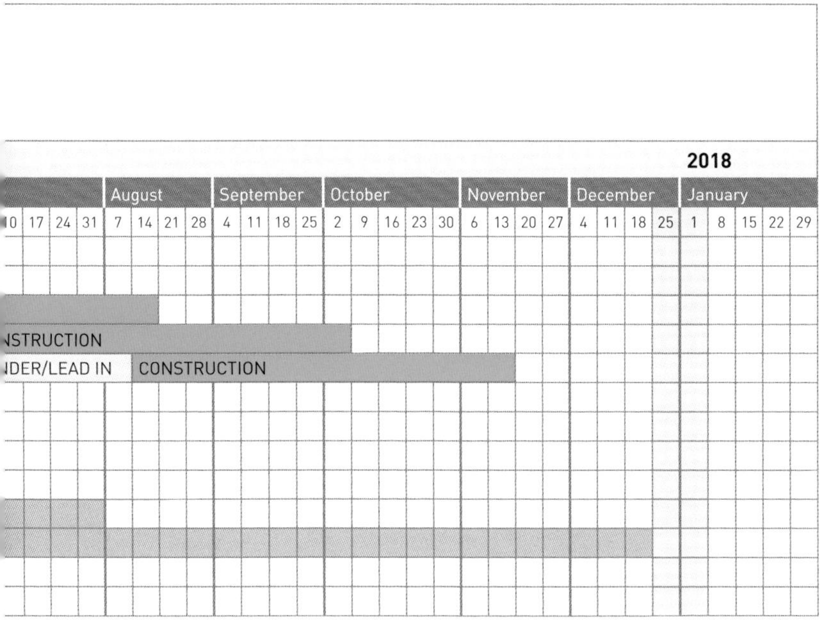

FIGURE 1.
Office workload
programme

periods blue, and so on. Keep it simple, and make sure it is always up to date. A quick glance at the programme can remind you of things that need to be done, such as checking whether a planning application has been approved, or that a tender is due back in a few days. (When your clients phone unexpectedly, they will expect you to have all this information at your fingertips!)

If your practice takes on projects as small as £50k, then in theory even a sole practitioner might be working on up to 15 jobs in any one year. If you can get a balance in the practice between a few small jobs and a few larger ones – say up to say £750k – it does make for a lot less information management, and fewer phone calls, emails, site visits and invoices to send out.

Expect all of the following:

- Your programme will be less streamlined than the simple version shown in Figure 1.
- The jobs will vary in size and length.
- A small, complex job requiring many approvals can sometimes take longer than a larger project that is more straightforward.
- Some jobs will be put on hold, for example to wait for planning approval.
- Some jobs will double in size during the pre-contract period, or even while on site.
- Some jobs will drag on long after they should have completed.
- You will have to grant extensions of time on some jobs.
- Things will also happen during the six-/12-month defects period.

The 'to do' list

As well as all the above programming, you will inevitably have a 'to do' list with all the admin tasks in the office, and all the tasks on each job that need to be done. I find it helpful, on a Friday afternoon while doing the backup, to update this list. This helps to clear your mind for the weekend, but also helps you to focus first thing Monday morning on what needs to be done, and in what order. It can also be your weekly reminder to check that invoicing is up to date.

Resourcing individual projects

Having agreed a percentage fee for a new project (see page 59–60), the next task is to break the fee down into stages and work out how many working hours are available at each stage. Probably the easiest way to explain how to do this is to give a simple example.

Work out how much it costs to employ the project architect including your time and overhead costs (holidays, sick, NI, pension, benefits, non-productive time, office costs, etc.). For a home office with low overheads, this might work out at salary of the architect multiplied by two, so if the architect is paid £25/hour the cost of the architect is £50/hour. In a larger office operating from rented premises this could be more.

Example

Contract budget: **£100,000** excl. VAT
Percentage fee 12% of £100,000 = **£12,000** (for basic architectural services)
Feasibility studies, dimensional survey, expenses, etc. to be charged separately on a time charge basis

> **STAGE 1**

Time charges will apply

> **STAGE 2**

(Concept Design, Developed Design)
35% of the total fee of £12,000 = **£4,200**
Cost of job architect, say £50/hour including overheads
£4,200/50 = **84** hours

> **STAGE 3**

(Technical Design – up to tender):
30% of the total fee of £12,000 = **£3,600**
£3,600/£50/hour = **72 hours**

> **STAGE 4**

(Technical Design – tender and appointment of a contractor):
5% of the total fee of £12,000 = £600
£600/£50/hour = **12 hours**

> **STAGE 5**

(Construction up to Practical Completion)
30% of the total fee of £12,000 = **£3,600**
£3,600/£50/hour = **72 hours**

> **STAGE 6**

(post-Practical Completion)
No fees for this stage, so ensure fees from previous stages cover this time.
Say 12 hours minimum

If the cost of the architect is £100/hour including overheads rather than £50/hour, adjust the hours accordingly. The architect who is paid twice as much has to do the same work in half the time.

The cost per hour of employing an architect will be based on the architect's salary and associated overheads, so by keeping the overheads low the amount of time spent working on projects can be increased, or you will be able to afford to allocate a more senior architect to the project.

Performance analysis

A quick review of time sheets can show how much time was spent on a project, and this can be compared with the project targets – but bear in mind that most small jobs grow at every stage, so if the budget has increased the time allowance must also increase. Also, it's not an exact science, so there's no need to spend hours making your analysis extremely detailed or accurate. It's enough for a small practice to have a rough idea.

If the time spent is greater than the time allocated at each stage check that you have the right architect on the job, how much they are paid and whether the work is being done efficiently. Check also that your overheads are not too high and query the level of fee that was agreed on the job – it might have been too low. Do not hold your employee responsible for losing money on the job if the fault is yours for agreeing a low fee or having high overheads. Also, if the job is not fully designed before it goes on site, this could give the impression that the early stages are profitable, but increase the amount of time needed later to produce further drawings.

How to avoid abortive work

Many architects fall into the trap of doing abortive work on domestic projects and not getting paid for it. Much of this work is because projects have gone over budget without the client's authorisation, and it can be avoided by keeping the client accurately informed at all stages about the likely cost of the project.

To reduce the risk of abortive work, architects should follow the RIBA Plan of Work and ensure that the design, brief and budget are confirmed at each stage of the project: Stages 1, 2, 3 and 4 (pre-tender estimate) and Stage 5 (estimated final accounts). If you, as the architect, do not have the skill to provide reasonable budget breakdowns and final account estimates of your projects, and there is no client-appointed quantity surveyor, you should employ a quantity surveyor or an estimator to do it for you. The return on your investment will be not only a better service for your client, but a reduced risk of doing abortive work. The other benefit of accurate budgeting during the project can be higher fees – if you are on a percentage fee then at each stage fee invoices will be based on the correct cost of the work, and not an underestimate.

> ON SMALL PROJECTS CLIENTS OFTEN CHANGE THE BRIEF
> THROUGHOUT THE PROJECT, WHICH MEANS THAT DURING
> CONSTRUCTION ITEMS ARE ADDED, SOMETIMES OMITTED,
> THEN ADDED BACK AGAIN. IT CAN BE TIME-CONSUMING
> TO KEEP UPDATING THE COST INFORMATION, BUT IT IS
> ESSENTIAL. AGAIN, IF YOUR FEE IS AN AGREED PERCENTAGE
> THEN IT IS CERTAINLY IN YOUR INTEREST TO BASE YOUR FEE
> ON THE LATEST BUDGET!

It is frustrating, costly and time-consuming for an architect to detail some fitted furniture or design the external works only to be told that these works are to be omitted to bring the scheme back in line with the agreed budget. Not only has the work been done for no fee, but the work also has to be undone for no fee. If a client wants fitted furniture and external works, these items should be added to the original brief and costed, and the cost agreed by the client before any design work is carried out. Clients usually agree to these extra costs if they are told about them when the items are added to the contract. If they do not agree to the extra cost, the architect will not do the work, so it does not matter.

All the above assumes that you were properly appointed in the first place, that a signed appointment document is in the job file, and that you did not do a lot of preliminary work in the hope of being appointed. If you do work for free in the hope that you will secure a commission, and you do not get the commission, then the cost of this abortive work must be offset against other jobs.

You will have informed your client in your appointment contract that certain works are outside your percentage fee and will be charged on an hourly basis. Examples include corresponding with adjoining owners, applying for a Thames Water build-over agreement, or protracted discussions around planning and multiple submissions to clear conditions. As soon as you are about to do the work for which you will charge on an hourly basis, inform your client, with an estimate of the hours involved, and get their agreement before you do the work. Otherwise there is a risk that they will say they thought the work was included in your percentage fee and refuse to pay the additional charges.

Reducing the risk of disputes and claims

Your practice should have an in-house procedure for dealing with complaints from clients, and a copy filed in the office manual so all employees are aware of the procedure. Try to deal with complaints before they become disputes or claims.

If you use the standard RIBA appointment contract, there will be provision within the agreement for the resolution of disputes. The choice will be between negotiation, mediation, adjudication or court proceedings. Arbitration on small projects is normally ruled out on cost grounds. However, all the options are expensive when compared to the fees you will charge on small projects, so always try to settle any hint of a complaint before it escalates into a dispute.

- If your client is justified in making a complaint, make sure the issue is resolved quickly and to their satisfaction and ensure that good relations are restored if there was any bad feeling.
- Confirm in writing to your client how the complaint was resolved and ask them to respond and confirm that the matter is settled to their satisfaction – and keep this correspondence on file.
- Never let a complaint remain unresolved until after Practical Completion.

- If the client complained about three things, make sure all three complaints are dealt with.
- If your client continues to complain, the situation could develop into a dispute or a claim against your practice, so let your insurers know and seek their advice.
- If you are a sole practitioner, discuss the situation with a colleague – they will be sympathetic, but distanced enough from the issue to give you good advice and support.

Some inexperienced clients make unreasonable demands of their architects and then complain that the architect is not providing the service they expect. Resolving this might just be a question of arranging a meeting and running through the services for which you have been appointed, and explaining that you are happy to undertake additional services on an hourly charge basis.

Other clients might wait until the job is on site, and then send long or frequent emails noting things they are not happy with, and/or making numerous changes to the brief. This is not a good way of communicating, and it can be a sign of future trouble. It might be wise to meet with your client to discuss any issues, allowing one hour for the meeting and issuing minutes. This positive step could be enough to make the client think twice about the number or the length of future emails.

Every practice runs the risk that a client will make a claim against it. The claim might be valid or spurious, but either way it will be stressful, expensive and time-consuming for you, and claims can drag on for many years. This is why you need a healthy balance in the company bank account, and why you have mandatory PI cover – and why it is crucial that the level of cover is adequate for each and every claim and includes all legal costs.

Be aware that many domestic clients also have legal cover included in their building and contents' insurance, so it will cost them nothing to claim against their architect or their builder. Sadly, there are clients who see this as a way of making easy money, and plenty of lawyers happy to pursue these claims as they make a good living from doing so. This practice is also on the increase, as our society becomes more claims conscious. For domestic clients, there is plenty of advice on Google about how to claim against your architect. This increased risk and the potential cost to the practice of a claim should be carefully weighed up and reflected in the practice fee income targets for each year.

If you think a client is going to make a claim, you must immediately notify your insurers. Your insurers or their lawyers will then advise you how to proceed, and they will not necessarily follow the dispute procedures in the appointment document you and your client have signed.

Here are some simple steps you can take to reduce the risk of claims and disputes:

- Pick your clients carefully. If you suspect they are going to be troublesome or litigious, it is best not to accept the commission.
- Have a formal appointment contract that states how disputes are to be dealt with. Go through it with your client and make sure it is signed before you do any work on the project.
- Ensure that any amendments to your appointment contract, such as a change in brief and associated costs, are also recorded and approved in writing by your client, and file the amendment with the original document.
- Ensure that the work you do is of a professional standard and complies with the RIBA Plan of Work. In particular make sure to provide your client with up-to-date budgets at all stages of the project and estimated final accounts during construction.
- Ensure any contractors' work that you certify is satisfactory and fully compliant with your specification. Defective work by a contractor can lead to a claim against the architect.
- Never over-certify the works on site.
- Arrange for variations to be priced in a timely manner, and agree these costs with your client, preferably before the work is done.
- If you advise your client to do something and they do not accept your advice, keep a record on file of the advice given and the reason the client gave for not accepting it (for example, to keep the cost down).

- If a client complains that something is not right, set up a meeting straight away and agree a reasonable solution. Confirm in writing what you have agreed. Keep a record on file of the discussion and the agreement.

- If you have signed up a client who seemed nice but turns out to be litigious or argumentative, or is inundating your office with emails and you start to have concerns, don't just ignore the signs. Keep a record on file of your contact with them, discuss with a colleague how you might deal with the situation, and get advice from your insurers or their lawyers if necessary. The earlier you take positive action, the more likely you are to resolve the issue before it escalates.

- Give your client the opportunity to explain any concerns they have and ask them what they see as the best solution to a particular problem.

- Try to resolve any issues and get confirmation from your client that the issue is resolved while the project is still on site, and that they want and need you to finish the job. Never agree to complete the contract and hand over the building with a view to resolving any issues after Practical Completion. At that point, the client has nothing to lose by making a claim – and everything to gain.

PEOPLE MANAGEMENT

The sole practitioner

Whether you are set up as a limited company or a sole trader, the sole practitioner architect is also the office manager and will need to do all of the following:

- Run the business.
- Keep abreast of relevant legislation, including the Building Regulations.
- Provide services as principal designer under the CDM Regulations.
- Outsource relevant tasks to others.
- Manage time, performance and risk.
- Organise people, information and tasks.
- Re-prioritise tasks on a daily basis.
- Arrange CPD training.
- Network and communicate well.
- Control cost and carry out value engineering on projects.
- Bring in work from the right kind of client.
- Handle difficult clients or contractors.
- Agree fees and ensure they are paid.
- Source good consultants, main contractors and specialist contractors.
- Keep abreast of building construction trends (current and historical).
- Design and detail buildings.
- Write specifications.
- Produce contract documentation.
- Carry out valuations and agree final accounts with contractors.
- Manage information technology (IT) in the office.

Despite the term 'sole practitioner' the job is very much about working with people, as on every project the architect is part of a team that includes the client, the consultants and the contractor. When working on a variety of small projects at the same time, the sole practitioner will spend a significant amount of time on the phone to clients, consultants, contractors, planners and building inspectors, and out of the office meeting existing and new clients and carrying out site visits.

Good health

Your health and your presence in the office during the week are important. Rather than struggle to work all day when you are coming down with something, it is better to immediately prioritise what must be done now and what can be left until later. Reschedule meetings if necessary, clear the urgent items, then leave the office to rest and recover – for a few days if necessary. If you are usually on top of everything and your contractors have all the information they need, and you are not holding up any payments, you will find that people will be sympathetic and will manage without you. It is best to avoid having meetings with clients if you are not well – you will not be at your best or make a good impression, and you might pass on a bug to your client. Most meetings can be re-scheduled.

Planning for an emergency

As a sole practitioner you will always have concurrent jobs at different stages, so you will need to plan for an emergency such as serious illness, accident or sudden death. You should have an emergency plan coordinated with your Will so your instructions on closing the practice can be followed through by your executors – see the section on emergency planning in Part 1. The emergency plan will ensure that your clients can be informed, and arrangements made for the projects in the office to be taken over by another practice.

FOR YOUR OWN PROTECTION YOU SHOULD ALSO CONSIDER TAKING OUT INCOME PROTECTION INSURANCE IN CASE OF SERIOUS INJURY OR ILLNESS.

Pension

Whether you have a limited company or operate as a sole trader, you should take advice and make arrangements for a personal private pension plan. Your accountant will be able to give you advice on any tax advantages available, depending on how your company is set up. One of the current advantages of being a company director of a limited company is that the company can make direct pension contributions into a director's personal pension fund before the calculation of Corporation Tax on the company profits. This is currently a tax-efficient way of saving into a pension fund. Always take current advice, however, as tax regimes change from year to year. The RIBA can also provide advice on pensions for architects.

Holidays and time off

The difficulty of taking a long holiday far away from the office is probably the worst thing about being a sole practitioner or running a very small office – but with good management and some flexibility, short holidays, time off and nice breaks are still possible. In a well-organised office, you should be able to go away for a week at a time without too much disruption, if you arrange everything in advance and let everyone know you will be away. If you cannot live without a long holiday every now and then, you will have to arrange cover.

Your PI insurers will require you to have emergency cover in place if you are not available or are out of the country on holiday. If you have a network of colleagues running similar practices, one of them should be able to provide this cover. Such an arrangement might be reciprocal, so you provide cover for them in return.

Backup from other consultants

Solicitor

A solicitor, like an accountant, can help in the setting up of a new company or partnership, or if you experience problems in the running or closing of the business and need advice. Even if you never have to employ a solicitor, it is comforting to have at least the name of one you can contact if the need arises. There are solicitors who specialise in construction law, and for certain queries you may need this specialist expertise. The Law Society can help you find the right solicitor.[10]

RIBA members will have access to 15 minutes per year of free legal telephone advice provided by a firm of London lawyers who provide advice to the RIBA and specialise in construction law. This small amount of time can often be enough to resolve a straightforward legal or contractual query on an individual project. Over my own years in practice, I have used this useful service on many occasions, and I have also attended many excellent CPD seminars at the same law firm.

Some (but not all) insurance companies that provide professional indemnity cover will employ their own in-house lawyers who can provide advice if you think a client might be going to make a claim against your practice. This type of legal advice is included in your policy premium.

If a claim is made against your practice, your insurers may appoint a firm of solicitors to deal with it. You will have no say in the selection of the solicitors. You will need to provide whatever information is requested, and the solicitors will provide you with advice on how best to respond to the claim.

Bank

The bank will be able to provide some advice on how to manage practice finances, and you should balance the value of this advice against the charges for the bank account. For a very small practice, it might be better to select a bank because the charges are low and get the advice you need from your accountant.

Insurance broker

You will need to find an insurance broker who specialises in professional indemnity insurance.

Remember that insurance brokers do not provide advice in the same way as solicitors or accountants, who are paid by you and act in your best interests. Brokers will obtain quotes for professional indemnity insurance cover from insurance companies, and are paid by the insurance companies. Insurance claims will be dealt with by the insurance company, not the insurance broker. The RIBA Insurance Agency offers professional indemnity insurance on terms agreed with the RIBA.

IT support

IT can be a challenge for the small office, so you must set up some form of support contract for times when you cannot deal with the inevitable issues and problems you will face. If possible, use a local IT support company who can send an engineer to the office if necessary, but can also remotely access the practice computers from their office.

It is a good idea to accept that we all have IT problems, which take time and money to resolve. You might need to allocate, say, three days a year to sorting out IT problems – and include an IT support budget in your cashflow forecast for the year (based on the amount you spent on IT in the previous year, if you have this figure). You will probably then find that the lost time is actually less than you anticipated.

When you do have an IT problem, years of experience have shown that the following simple procedure often works: don't panic. Close all your work documents and clear your desk. Close the computer and have a cup of tea and ten minutes away from your desk. Then turn everything back on and – amazingly – 50% of the time things will be working again! If you still have a problem, the short break and the cup of tea will sustain you while you try to figure out a solution before calling your IT support company. If you are conscientious about backing up daily, you will not have the added worry of losing more than a few hours' work.

Website designer

Some small practices set up their own websites and use their own photographs, but these tend to look less professional and it might be a false economy. It will take a long time to produce your own website, and you will not get the same result you would with something by a good, professional designer.

There are hundreds of excellent websites for architectural practices, so you can learn a huge amount by just going online and looking at them. Finding the right web designer for you can be a bit more challenging. If you can find a person who can come to your office not just during the design stage, but to update the site for you, this is ideal. Everything can be done remotely these days, but sometimes a face-to-face meeting with a fellow designer is more productive and enjoyable.

Photographer

Commission the best photographer you can afford and, if possible, use the same photographer for all your projects so there is consistency of style across photographs. This is not just good for your website – it is good for your own morale to have excellent photographs of the work into which you will have put so much care, time and effort. Your clients will also be happy to show these photos to their friends and family and on social media, and this is where your next job might come from. It will also be easier to have your work published if you have good photos.

Just be sure to agree copyright issues and permissions with the photographer in advance before using or publishing the photos. Keep a record of these permissions on file.

Quantity surveyor

On larger contracts, a quantity surveyor (QS) will be appointed direct by the client, but on small contracts where no quantity surveyor is appointed it may still be a necessary to get some help from one with budgets or even final accounts, and paying for this on an hourly charge basis. You might need just a few hours at key stages. If you do not have the skill to produce detailed budgets and pre-tender estimates, you will have no choice but to appoint a quantity surveyor or arrange for the appointment of a QS by the client.

Design team consultants

Even the smallest project might necessitate the appointment of various consultants, including:

- structural engineer
- quantity surveyor
- services engineer
- party wall surveyor
- acoustic consultant
- audio-visual (AV) consultant
- private building inspector (if local authority inspector not used).

Your clients will probably expect you to decide what services the consultants should provide and to arrange for quotes. It is quite rare for domestic clients to want to use consultants other than the ones their architect recommends, though they might on occasion want more than one quote or they may know a particular consultant they want to use. You can speak to consultants on the phone to see if they can take on a job before sending them all the details and asking them to provide a quote for their services. Quotes from consultants should be sent direct to the client, and consultants should be appointed by the client. Invoices from consultants should also be sent direct to the client, even if they are copied to you for checking and authorising. Remember that your PI insurer will insist that the consultants you work with also carry professional indemnity insurance.

If you are doing the same kind of work in the same geographical area for many years, you may be fortunate enough to work repeatedly with the same consultant QS, structural engineer or services engineer or party wall surveyor. These colleagues, along with your network of other small practices, with whom you have an ongoing relationship, can be invaluable when you need five minutes of telephone advice. The arrangement has to be mutual though, so you should be prepared to help others with their queries too. While we have had any number of IT support companies and arrangements over the years as technology has evolved, we have worked for many years with the same accountant, bookkeeper, website designer, quantity surveyor, structural engineer and party wall surveyor. Their advice and support have been invaluable.

It is a good idea to have a contact sheet for each project with contact details for all the consultants, and to circulate this to all parties involved. Domestic clients will often ring the practice years after their project is completed to ask for a structural engineer's name or telephone number, or to help with a query on a fitting specified by a consultant, so it's a good idea to have these contact sheets to hand afterwards, too.

Employing staff

Growing the practice and taking on staff can be rewarding, and allows the practice to bring in new skills and talent, use resources more efficiently, and be more flexible about taking on larger or more challenging projects. However, careful planning is necessary, especially if you have not employed staff before, as office and IT systems, pension arrangements and your PAYE system might all need to change. You might also have to move to larger office premises.

- Some practices accept that they will grow and shrink as their workload expands and contracts. This is probably more common in the larger practices, where key staff can always be retained.
- Some practices grow to a certain size and then decide to stay at that size.
- Some practices want to stay small, and they are happy to buy in support or take on temporary staff to cope with peaks in workload.

If you are currently a sole practitioner and are taking on staff for the first time you must check current employment legislation,[11] notify your PI insurers, speak to the practice accountant for advice and consider the following for each new employee:

- contract terms
- job description
- induction
- targets
- performance management
- salary and performance reviews

- holidays
- sick leave
- CPD
- pension
- workplace and workstation
- health and safety
- PAYE and National Insurance
- employers' liability insurance.

You accountant may be able to advise you on employment legislation, such as your obligation to enrol your employees into a workplace pension, and on employment issues generally, including redundancy and dismissal procedures.

Employee qualifications and experience

When writing a job description, you must decide what level of qualifications and experience your new employee will need, and the appropriate salary level, bearing in mind what the practice can afford to pay. It is a luxury you probably cannot afford to employ someone who is over-skilled for the job, but it is also a false economy to employ someone who is under-skilled, as they will not be able to work independently and might make mistakes that you will then need to rectify. Also, the less skilled an employee is, the more likely it is that you will spend a lot of your time training them, and this will reduce your own productivity. As with everything in the small practice, it is important to get the balance right.

Resource and performance analysis

As soon as the practice employs more than one person, the allocation of resources and performance analysis will become more important. Employing junior employees will allow the senior employees to focus on the more challenging tasks in the office, while junior staff will take on the tasks appropriate to their skill level, making more efficient use of resources. How to allocate resources to a project is covered in detail on page 101.

Full- or part-time staff/Long- or short-term contract

The workload in a small practice varies, so it is good to be aware of the possibility of employing full-time or part-time staff on either a permanent or a short-term contract. The ability of the practice to bring in new staff will also depend on the office accommodation, as each new person will require a proper workstation and a minimum amount of space.

Employee career development

A challenge that every small practice will face is career development for employees, so that each individual feels they have a future within the practice. If you employ someone who needs a lot of training and supervision, once they have developed their skills they may seek better-paid work elsewhere and leave. You will therefore need to find ways to encourage good employees to stay with the practice, such as increasing responsibility, regular performance and salary reviews, and other benefits such as specialist training, a good pension scheme, or providing lunch or flexible working hours.

When employing new staff and deciding on the most suitable candidate, think not just about what work needs to be done immediately, but how both you and the candidate feel about the longer term. If you have a very small practice, then the experienced architect returning to work after parental leave with a child at a local primary school and wanting to work part-time might be more suited to your practice than the ambitious young architect who will want to work full-time but may leave after a relatively short period, forcing you to go through the costly and time-consuming recruitment process again.

Outsourcing

Sometimes it makes sense to employ consultants rather than trying to do everything in-house. While this can seem expensive, it does enable you to access skills on an 'as needed' basis. The consultants you might employ, who will charge the practice for their services on an hourly charge basis, are an accountant, a bookkeeper, a quantity surveyor, a website designer, a photographer, an IT support company and CAD survey company (for more about working with consultants, see page 110).

It is possible to employ architectural staff through an agency, but this is expensive and should only be considered as a short-term solution when no other option is available.

Work/life balance

The best way of working is the way that suits your needs and preferences. These will vary from one individual to another and at different stages in your career. What has worked well for me is running a small architectural practice from home. It was the only way I could continue to work full-time and be sure that my daughter never came home from school to an empty house. The house is quiet during the day and is large enough for me to use the loft level as an office, and I enjoy working on small projects. Working from home means no commuting, so it's possible to work an eight- or nine-hour day and still have time to go for a swim in the morning before work, and to be in the kitchen preparing dinner five minutes after closing the office.

Sleep

Architects hold a lot of information in their head, and proper sleep allows the brain to organise and logically store all the information gathered during the course of the day. To stay up all night trying to meet a deadline (and what architect has not done this?) is rarely worth it, as productivity the next day will be likely to drop.

Good food

Lunch and a proper break away from the office in the middle of the day to take a short walk will keep you going a lot longer than a rushed sandwich at your desk.

Exercise

The best way to keep fit when your work forces you to work at a desk all day is to find a form of regular exercise you like. It could be the gym or swimming or cycling or running. What I enjoy is dancing, because when you are on a dance floor it is impossible to think about work – it is mental relaxation, a bit of socialising and physical exercise all in one.

Holiday, working hours and flexibility

Limit the hours that you work to a reasonable level, and take breaks. If you are a sole practitioner, it is difficult to take long holidays without making arrangements for cover, but you can often take days off or work shorter days when the office is not busy. For some, this year-round flexibility may be preferable to working flat-out nearly all year and then taking a few weeks off. For staff members with small children, it will be important to enable flexible working hours to fit around childcare.

If possible, holidays should be undisturbed by emails and texts about work.

Work/life balance review

The success of your practice depends on the people it employs, and their wellbeing and loyalty are critical. It is a good idea to consider the work/life balance of your staff as part of the yearly review, even if you are a sole practitioner. If members of staff or sole practitioners are constantly working long hours, or feeling stressed and not taking time out, this could be an indication that the practice is taking on too much work, or that the work is not being undertaken efficiently, or that the fees are too low for the work involved, or the office overheads or salaries are too high, or a combination of these things. These should be checked and addressed before a problem develops that affects someone's health or happiness, or the viability of the practice.

Training and continuing professional development (CPD)

The basic CPD requirement for an architect is 35 hours of learning per year/100 learning points, regardless of what stage you are at in your career and whether you work for a large or a small practice, or as a sole practitioner. You should plan this training carefully as it will take up a lot of time, especially if the courses are not in-house – you might need to travel a long way, even for a one-hour session. Make sure the courses you attend are relevant to your needs and the work of the practice. Every architect should keep their own record of training courses attended.

CPD categories

1. Health and safety (two hours per year is mandatory)
2. Professional context
   - architectural design
   - sustainable architecture.
3. Practice management
   - business administration
   - employment legislation
   - marketing and selling
   - Quality Management (QM) systems
   - risk management
   - staff management
   - taxation, finance and VAT
   - time and resource management.
4. Managing projects
   - engagement of an architect
   - brief development
   - procurement and building contracts
   - building cost management
   - project management

- risk management
- dispute resolution
- facilities management.

5. Construction skills
  - technical innovations
  - specification writing
  - choosing materials
  - statutory requirements
  - cross-professional knowledge.

6. Personal skills development
  - communication skills
  - IT skills
  - client management.

Many of the above topics will be covered during the CPD day of the RIBA Small Practice Conference or other CPD days at the RIBA.

Some CPD sessions are provided, free of charge, by other architectural practices or consultants, including lawyers and structural engineers. You can contact the consultants you work with and ask to be included on their list of invitees.

If you want to do a particular CPD course, such as structural glazing or basement tanking, you can contact specialist firms and ask if they will be doing any presentations in the near future, preferably local to your office. If they are, they can arrange for you to attend.

Many CPD sessions are paid for by product manufacturers or specialist contractors, and sessions can often be arranged during a lunch break in your own office. Small practices doing similar work can benefit hugely from sharing these CPD sessions, as they can then be specifically tailored to the work these practices do. Providers usually ask for a minimum of 10–12 attendees, and they usually offer to pay for refreshments.

Increasingly, CPD is being offered in the form of webinars, and this is extremely efficient as you can choose those that are best suited to your CPD needs. The speakers are often skilled and senior people, and no time is lost travelling.

Health and safety – first-aiders

To comply with the Health and Safety at Work Act, every company must have a first-aider in the office. The one-day courses for first-aiders run by St John Ambulance at its premises are excellent practical courses, and good value.

Working with domestic clients

Whoever they are, your clients are key to making your business a success and profitable – so it is important that you understand them, look after them and meet their expectations over and above providing the architectural services they have commissioned.

The typical domestic client

Working with domestic clients – or any clients on small, one-off projects – is quite different from working with commercial clients. Domestic clients can be any age, from 20 to 90. They might be wealthy or struggling to make ends meet. They might be an architect, or a professional in another field, or a business entrepreneur, or retired. They might be any nationality, and might not speak English well or even live in the UK. They might be eccentric, or suffering from a medical condition, or disabled, or neurotic, or so busy at work you hardly ever meet them. And on top of all this, a domestic client is rarely one person. More often than not it will be a couple, or even two couples living side by side. We had a project in the office some years ago where the client was a woman at the beginning of the project and had changed gender to become a man by Practical Completion.

Domestic projects tend to be relatively small, so even in a small office you are likely to have many projects running at the same time, and as many individual clients from all the above walks of life. On some refurbishment projects, the clients will remain in the property during construction. You must get to know clients quickly and sufficiently well to be able to design and work on their homes, and to help them enjoy the project even if the budget is tight, there's dust everywhere and they had not realised how noisy and stressful it would be to live on a building site.

What domestic clients want and expect from their architect and how much they will involve themselves and influence the design of their project will vary hugely. This is part of the challenge and the enjoyment of doing domestic work – but you, and your contractors, really do need to understand people and enjoy working with them. A good sense of humour helps.

The ideal client

The ideal client will like what you have already achieved. They will readily confirm your appointment and agree your fees without trying to negotiate a reduction. They will give you a realistic brief, agree a realistic budget and take your professional advice on all matters throughout the project. They will let you get on with the project, only meeting and corresponding as necessary. They will approve the design and budget and pay invoices without delay. They will get on well with the contractors, and allow you to photograph the property for your website. They will recommend you to all their friends and tell them they love what you have done and how you have done it.

If only it were always like this!

The difficult client

Some very nice people – they might even be your family or friends – can make difficult clients. Some clients, for example, cannot fix their brief. Others will be convinced that you should be able to do the project for less than the budget you recommend. Some will want to design the project themselves, and it can take a long time to persuade them that their design ideas may not work. Others will want to use a contractor they know for all the wrong reasons. such as he'll give them a good price if they pay in cash! Some are only available for meetings on Sunday mornings or after 9pm on weekdays. Others still will send long emails on a daily basis, or make long phone calls, or want to meet on site twice a week. All these issues are common with domestic work, and as long as the clients are reasonable people it is still usually possible to establish a good working relationship. You may have to give these projects a bit more time and be flexible about the hours you work – but be careful: if one client takes up an excessive amount of your time, it is unlikely you will make any profit on the project. You could also be distracted from other more profitable projects in the office.

The problem client

Most architects who carry out domestic work over a number of years will have a story about the one client they wish they had never met. Problems usually revolve around a client's reluctance to part with their money, and might include some or all of the following:

- The client who is reluctant to agree the terms in your appointment contract and wants to negotiate a reduction in your fee.
- The client who argues that your advice on budget is wrong and insists the project should cost less.
- The client who refuses to appoint a quantity surveyor when the scope of work or level of complexity warrants the appointment.
- The client who wants to design the project instead of providing a brief and allowing the architect to come up with a design to meet it.
- The client who claims they did not understand they had to pay for additional services, even when it is clear in the appointment contract.
- The couple client where both parties give conflicting instructions on budget and brief – e.g. one asks for additional work while the other insists the budget is fixed.
- The client who constantly changes the brief but refuses to accept any additional charge for abortive work.
- The client who takes up excessive amounts of your time throughout the project with phone calls, emails and meetings.
- The client who instructs the operatives on site without consulting the architect or even the main contractor, but then refuses to accept the additional cost or responsibility for any consequences of the instruction.
- The client who pays every invoice late and only after reminders are issued.
- The client who wants to purchase materials direct to save money, but refuses to accept responsibility if the goods arrive late or damaged.
- The client who tries to arrange private meetings with the contractor and makes cash deals to avoid paying VAT.
- The client who holds you responsible for any defects in the contractor's work, but will not allow the contractor to remedy them.
- The client who finds fault with your work or the contractor's work to justify withholding payment, and counterclaims if you take any action.

Even if the practice needs work it is better to turn down a commission from such clients if you suspect this behaviour is likely before your appointment is confirmed. The experience will be unpleasant, a lot of your time will be wasted, and it is unlikely that the project will make a profit.

Unless you are very lucky, it is possible that you will sign up one or two problem clients over the life of the practice. Never underestimate how damaging such clients can be to the practice, and how difficult and unpleasant it will be to see these jobs through. Keep a note on the project file of any warning signs. Make sure your documentation and records are thorough, and keep records of conversations and phone calls. Confirm everything you discuss with your clients by email, even if it means the archives for these jobs are twice the size of your normal files. Contact your insurers if you think the client is going to make a claim and get advice.

Some excellent free legal advice is available to RIBA members, and your insurers may also employ lawyers who can provide advice. You can also discuss and agree with a colleague the best strategy for dealing with your difficult client. This could be another architect or perhaps the project quantity surveyor who knows the client. Your colleague may be able to offer objective advice. If you have a good strategy for dealing with the situation, and you tread carefully and cautiously through the project, you have a much better chance of surviving the ordeal. It can at best be a learning experience!

Always resolve any client issues or complaints prior to Practical Completion when the client still needs you on board to complete the project. Make sure your invoices are up to date and based on an accurate estimate of the final account, and paid on time, so the amount owing after Practical Completion is minimal. This is good practice generally, but vital if you are dealing with a client who you suspect is trying every trick in the book to short change you or the contractor.

Selecting clients

**ARCHITECTS SHOULD SELECT THEIR CLIENTS AS
CAREFULLY AS CLIENTS SELECT THEIR ARCHITECT.**

Deciding which clients to accept are among the most important decisions you will make (along with selecting contractors, see page 171), and the success of your practice will depend to a large extent on these decisions.

Carrying out a preliminary site consultation on an hourly charge basis is a good way of getting to know a client before taking on the full project.

Charging your clients

There is no reason to do any work for free on domestic projects. If you charge properly for your work, your clients will probably respect you and value the work more than if you do it for nothing. You will also make more money!

Tips for working with domestic clients

- Ensure that a signed copy of your appointment contract is in the job file before you do any work on the project.
- If you are going to do a few hours on an hourly charge basis prior to confirmation of your appointment, confirm this in writing with your client and ask them to countersign a copy of the letter or confirm by email. Make it clear what you are going to do and how many hours you estimate, then don't go over this without approval. Make sure your invoice is paid before you accept the full commission.
- Go to the first client meeting with an agenda (this can be a standard agenda you use on every project), so you remember what questions to ask and what information to check on site. Take a camera and a calculator with you, as clients will expect you to provide guidance on cost.
- Before the first meeting, ask your client to prepare a brief and a portfolio of images they like, along with any drawings, surveys or reports they might have. They can do this with magazine images, or digitally using sites such as Houzz.com.

- Be a good listener – if you are dealing with a couple, listen carefully to both parties. They might not be saying the same thing! If they obviously do not agree on the some aspect of the brief or budget, help them reach a consensus or suggest they email you with a joint decision after the meeting. Write up your notes straight after the meeting.

- Be observant – if the meeting is in the client's house, look carefully at the furniture, the appliances, the light fittings, the artwork, the décor, their books, their gadgets, the garden. Are they tidy, or is there stuff all over the place? The car they drive, the clothes they are wearing and so on will all tell you a lot about the kind of people they are and how they live, the type of project they will expect and how much they are likely to spend.

- Give new clients a copy of a previous pre-contract programme so they can see and understand how a project progresses through the various stages and approvals. This is also a good opportunity to show them at what point you will be submitting fee invoices, when valuations will be done during construction, and how often you will visit the site.

- Be prepared to not accept a commission if you do not think the client will be easy to work with, even if the project is interesting.

- Be prepared to not accept a commission if the project is not one you want for the practice, even if the clients are nice people. Don't underestimate how difficult this can be, especially if it's a word-of-mouth recommendation or a friend.

- Tell clients that even if they want to use their old appliances or fittings, your fee will reflect the value of new ones. Also, warn them that the contractor will not guarantee the performance of reused appliances or sanitary fittings, or appliances and fittings they purchase direct. It's best that all orders come through the main contractor due to the risks of client direct orders.

- Be prepared to give a bit more time to jobs where you have a difficult client. Sometimes that's all it takes to make it a successful, rather than a stressful project.

- If a client is difficult in the early stages they will probably be difficult the whole way through the project (which could take years), so try to spot the early signs of a potentially difficult client and turn down the commission or develop a strategy to manage the situation.

- A good way of making sure you are paid for client-requested design changes during Stages 2–6 is to agree a percentage fee for the whole project. Clients can also easily keep track of estimated total final cost if they simply add the fee percentage to every estimated final account. (For more about fee structures, see pages 59–60.)

- Be prepared to run some checks on your clients before signing a contract.

- Work hard to extract a proper brief from your client for the project. Confirm the written brief with the client and reissue it with revisions as they occur. The final brief is nearly always very different to the one agreed at the appointment stage.

- Give good budget advice at inception and then at every stage of the project. Get budget approval at each stage before moving to the next stage.

- Time-charge for feasibility studies and any services where you cannot estimate in advance. For example, party wall matters, or prolonged exchanges of correspondence around planning issues. Agree an estimate of the time this will take with your client; don't go over the estimate without further agreement.

- Keep records of what you tell your clients. This may be crucial later on if a client claims you did not tell them something important.

- A domestic client will rarely have any experience of working with an architect, and little idea of what an architect does. Your website can give a new client a lot of information about what the practice does, but you will also have to explain at a meeting what you do, and go through your appointment contract with them, explaining anything that they do not understand.

- Rather than wait until the end of the project to get feedback from your clients, ask for it at each stage of the project, so if there are any issues they can be addressed straight away. Ask you clients if they are happy with progress and the information provided, including budget advice. Check that your clients are happy at each stage, then issue an invoice and make sure it is paid before you release information relating to the next stage.

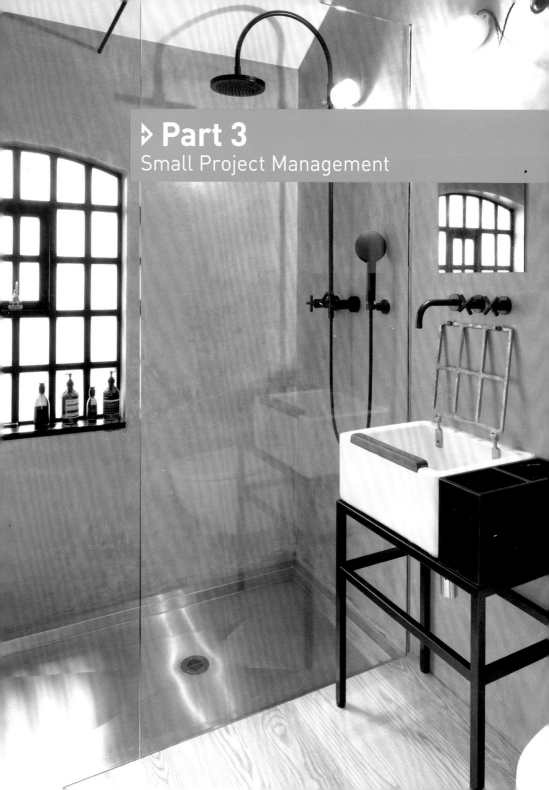

▷ Part 3
Small Project Management

RIBA Plan of Work

In 2013 the RIBA published a new Plan of Work, with Stages 0–7 replacing the old RIBA Work Stages A–L. The Plan of Work details the tasks and outputs required at key stages of a project from inception to completion. On small and domestic projects services are not normally required at Stages 0 and 7.

The Plan of Work is a free digital document available online from the RIBA.[12] It can be made practice-specific and the type of procurement can be selected, so the plan can be tailored for an individual project or become the office standard Plan of Work.

For the small practice taking on small projects and working almost exclusively with domestic clients it is highly likely that you will be using traditional procurement[13] for all projects. You might find it useful to produce a practice-specific Plan of Work, fusing traditional procurement with information relating to fees for each stage, as shown in Figure 2. A digital copy of the Plan of Work on your desktop or a printed copy on the wall beside your desk is a helpful reminder of what you should be doing at each stage of a project, and what information to produce before a stage is complete and you can invoice.

Project plan

A project plan is a project-specific development of the Plan of Work. It will contain information relating to drawings, documents and procedures for each stage of the project. On a domestic project it might be sufficient to use the Plan of Work and a detailed pre-contract programme.

Consistency

Consistency in your approach to office administration and project management generally is the key to efficient performance in the small office. If the practice has a lot of small jobs in the office at the same time, and all the jobs follow the same Plan of Work and fee invoices are sent out in line with the work stages, this will speed up administration. If you use the same Plan of Work, the same construction contract, the same version of the NBS specification, the same tender document format, and so on, you will become familiar with these documents and more efficient at putting them together.

FEE	TIME CHARGE	TIME CHARGE	15%	35%
WORK STAGES	**0** PROJECT REQUIREMENTS	**1** PROJECT BRIEF	**2** CONCEPT DESIGN	**3** DEVELOPED DESI
CORE OBJECTIVES	Identify: Client's Brief Client's Budget Client's Programme	Initial Project Brief Collect Site Information Feasibility Studies Develop Project Budget Outline Programme	Final Project Brief Concept Design including Structural and M+E Outline Specification Preliminary Cost Information Pre Contract Programme	Developed Design inclu Structural and M+E an Specialists Outline Specification Updated Cost Informati Pre Contract Programm Party Wall Matters defir
SUSTAINABILITY	Sustainability checkpoint 0	Sustainability checkpoint 1	Sustainability checkpoint 2	Sustainability checkpoir
PROCUREMENT	Project Team - initial considerations	Architect appointment confirmed Consultant appointments confirmed		Quotes from specialist subcontractors if applic
PROGRAMME				Pre Contract Programm
PLANNING BUILDING REGULATIONS		Pre application discussion if applicable	Pre application discussion if applicable Outline Planning Application if applicable	Submit Planning Applic
CDM		Inform client of their duties Principal Designer appointed	Pre construction information collected Risk Assessment	Pre construction information collected Risk Assessment
KEY SUPPORT TASKS		CAD survey of existing building Project Execution Plan agreed including Information Exchanges and Communication		
INFORMATION EXCHANGE	Client's Preliminary Brief Client's Preliminary Budget Available Site Information	Initial Project Brief Initial Project Budget Initial Project Programme Project Team details Existing Site Information CAD Survey of Existing Building Feasibility Study(ies)	Final Brief Concept Design drawings including Structural and M+E Outline Specification Preliminary Cost Infomation Preliminary Programme	Developed design drawi including Structural and M+E design and special Outline Specification Updated Cost Informatic Updated Programme
LEVEL OF DETAIL		Feasibility Study	1:1250 Location Plan 1:500 Site Plan 1:100 Plans, Sections and Elevations	1:1250 Location Plan 1:500 Site plan 1:100 Plans, Sections ar Elevations 1:50 Sketch details Detailed specification
FEEDBACK		Client feedback and agreement to proceed to Stage 2	Client feedback and agreement to proceed to Stage 3	Client feedback and agreement to proceed to Stage 4

FIGURE 2

65% (OUT TO TENDER) 70% (CONTRACTOR APPOINTED)	100%	INCL IN % FEE	TIME CHARGE
4 **TECHNICAL DESIGN**	**5** **CONSTRUCTION**	**6** **HANDOVER**	**7** **IN USE**
...nical Design including Structural, ... and Specialist subcontractor ...ign ...y coordinated Specification ...der Documents ...y Wall Agreements ...Tender Estimate	Construction Issue drawings Off Site Manufacture On Site Construction Resolution of design queries from site	Hand over building Final Account agreed Defects Inspection Issue Final Certificate	
...ainability checkpoint 4	Sustainability checkpoint 5	Sustainability checkpoint 6	Sustainability checkpoint 7
...e tenders ...lyse tenders ...int Main Contractor ...contract meeting	Administration of the Building Contract to Practical Completion Site inspections	Conclude administration of the Building Contract	Maintain relationship with client and provide in use services as appointed
...contract programme ...struction programme	Contract construction programme monitor progress		
...ication for Building Regs Plans ...roval ...er submissions requiring consent ...ning conditions cleared	Outstanding planning conditions cleared Building Regs Completion Certificate		
...Construction Information issued ...tender ...cipal Contractor appointed ...provides Construction Phase Plan	Construction Phase Plan developed Information for the Health and Safety File collected	Handover of 'latest construction issue' or 'as-built' drawings Health and Safety File	
...se on contractor selection and ...ract selection ...are the Contract and arrange for ...ing ...se client on responsibilities under ...Contract and Contract Insurances		Update project information as required	Post Occupancy Evaluation
...pleted technical design and ...cification ...der Documents ...der Analysis and Reccommendation	Construction issue drawings Interim Valuations and Interim Certificates Draft Final account Site Instructions	'Latest construction issue' drawings or 'as-built' information The Health and Safety File The Building Manual (Guarantees etc.) Final account	
...0 Block Plan ...0 Site Plan including drainage, ...rnal works ...Plans, Sections, Elevations ...Detailed Plans and Sections ..., 1:5 Full size component details ...-/window/finishes/sanitary fittings/ ...t fittings Schedules ...cialist subcontractor design ...ailed Specification	As Stage 4	1:100 Site Plan including drainage etc 1:50 Plans, Sections, Elevations Structural drawings Specialist subcontractor drawings Schedules Services drawings	
...nt feedback and agreement ...roceed to Stage 5	Client feedback and agreement to issue Practical Completion and proceed to Stage 6	Client feedback	Client feedback

Use the Plan of Work to help you invoice

Before sending out an invoice at any particular stage to a client, check the Plan of Work first to be sure that not only drawings, but updated specifications, budget and programme have also been issued, sustainability and health and safety checks made, and submissions and approvals obtained. Then check that your client is happy with everything and ready to proceed to the next stage. Only then send out your invoice, confident that your client is aware of what work the invoice relates to and is happy with the work you have done.

The architect's appointment

Contracts are mandatory

The ARB Architects Code: Standards of Conduct and Practice[14] and the RIBA Code of Conduct[15] both state that all appointment contracts must be explained, understood and agreed with your clients and confirmed in writing. However, all too often the terms are not agreed and the documents are not signed before some early-stage work commences on the project. Pending formal appointment, many clients expect their architect to attend meetings or provide ideas and advice for free, hoping that the carrot of a new project is sufficient reward. The same clients do not expect their lawyers, plumbers or hairdressers to visit their properties and work for free (it's highly unlikely they would), but somehow architects – despite all the liability they carry – are fair game. If you are providing services in advance of appointment for the full project, it should be on a pre-agreed basis, such as for an hourly charge.

Small projects

It is a mistake to think that a very small project does not warrant a proper appointment contract. Small projects such as a basement extension to an existing house, or even a loft conversion, are the very ones where problems are most likely to occur. A small domestic project can also develop into a larger project halfway through the design, or even when the project is on site, so it is good practice to set up all projects in a consistent way with an appropriate appointment contract.

Consistency

If your practice does one medium-sized project a year you can afford to spend some time selecting or tailoring the appointment contract with your client, as the amount of time you spend doing this relative to the fee income on the project is not significant. However, if your practice takes on lots of small projects you may have to prepare ten or fifteen appointment contracts in a year. For this reason, it is a good idea to make the contract you use consistent across all your projects so you are familiar with the contract and new versions can be prepared, signed and filed quickly and efficiently, allowing you to get on with the design work.

Getting the contract signed

The first bit of paperwork in a new project file should be the signed contract confirming your appointment. No work should be done on a project until the signed contract is in the project file. If a client arranges for a few hours' work on an hourly charge basis prior to a more formal appointment, this should be confirmed in an email to which the client is invited to respond and accept, so you have written confirmation of your appointment.

Forms of contract

The contract with your client for a new project can be the standard RIBA appointment contract, or a contract you have drawn up specifically for your practice. Your insurers may prefer that you use the RIBA documents, as these have been carefully worded to provide protection for both the client and the architect. You must ensure that your clients fully understand the terms they are agreeing to, and in particular the clauses that relate to dispute resolution and professional indemnity insurance.

The RIBA produces a range of appointment contracts and these are updated every five years or so.

The contracts you are most likely to use on small projects are as follows:

DOMESTIC PROJECTS

- RIBA Domestic Professional Services Contract 2017, or
- RIBA Domestic Project Agreement (2012 edition), or
- RIBA Guide to letter contracts (2012) – for projects under £100,000.

NON-DOMESTIC PROJECTS

- RIBA Concise Professional Services Contract 2017, or
- RIBA Concise Agreement (2012 edition), or
- RIBA Guide to letter contracts (2012) – for projects under £100,000.

 A 'DOMESTIC PROJECT' IS A PROJECT WHERE THE CLIENT IS A DOMESTIC CLIENT AND THE PROJECT IS THEIR MAIN HOME. A NON-DOMESTIC PROJECT IS A PROJECT FOR A BUILDING THAT IS NOT THE CLIENT'S MAIN HOME.

Letter contracts are only suitable for small, straightforward projects. Further guidance on the use of letter contracts can be found in the RIBA Guide to Letter Contracts, and a standard format can be downloaded from the RIBA Bookshop free of charge.[16]

Risk

If you provide services to clients without a written and signed contract, or if a contract is not updated when circumstances change, you run the risk of not being paid for part or all of the work done. It is worth remembering that clients who drag their feet in signing a contract or agreeing to revisions to the budget are the very ones who might not pay, especially if the project is a feasibility study and does not go ahead, or if a project is not granted planning permission. Any court action to recover outstanding fees would stand little chance of winning if there was no written and signed agreement on fees.

How to charge for Stage 1 work

Few clients would want to sign a contract with an architect for a new project prior to some initial discussion, a visit to the site and some guidance on budget, so it is important to provide a preliminary consultation. This advice should be provided at your client's expense and not yours.

What might work well for a small practice receiving regular enquiries about domestic projects is to have a standard procedure for dealing with, and charging for, preliminary enquiries, as follows:

- Initial enquiry by phone or email – call might last 15–30 minutes – **no charge.**
- Invite client to 30-minute meeting at the office to make face-to-face contact and to see the work of the practice – **no charge** (after 30 minutes **apply hourly charge**).
- Preliminary site consultation including travel, site visit, taking client's brief and discussing the budget, follow-up with written report with confirmation of client's brief and more detailed advice on budget, consultants' fees and other costs and programme – for a domestic project, depending on travel, this will usually be 2–4 hours' work – **hourly charge.**

After the first phone call, an email can be sent to the new client confirming your terms, the hourly charge rate and what services can be provided on this basis until a more formal appointment is agreed.

For a new client the cost of 2–4 hours' work by an architect is an excellent investment and should help them to move from a vague idea of what they want, with little idea of what it costs, to having a good understanding of what the project will involve, how much it will cost, how long it will take and how an architect will help them through the process.

Your clients will be more likely to prepare carefully for the meeting and less likely to waste your time if they are paying you on an hourly charge basis.

EXPLAIN YOUR CHARGES.

IF YOU MAKE IT CLEAR AT APPOINTMENT STAGE WHAT INFORMATION WILL BE ISSUED AT EACH STAGE, WHAT YOUR CHARGES WILL BE FOR EACH STAGE, WHEN YOUR CLIENTS CAN EXPECT A FEE INVOICE, AND APPROXIMATELY HOW MUCH IT WILL BE, THEN YOU ARE MUCH MORE LIKELY TO GET A PROMPT SETTLEMENT.

Revisions to the appointment contract

The architect's appointment contract is usually prepared and sent out after the first consultation meeting, but the brief and budget recorded in the documents are likely to change as the project develops at each stage. At the end of each stage, check the brief and the budget and email your client to check that they are happy to accept any additional cost before proceeding to the next stage. Keep a copy of the emails and the client's responses with the original appointment document. Never allow your client to say that the cost of the project increased without their consent, or that the brief was altered without their consent. Keeping your client informed of the brief and the budget and their agreement will ensure that you do not have to do any abortive work and your fees will always be based on the latest estimate.

Revisions to the appointment contract – Stages 0–7

RIBA STAGE	ITEM
0 STRATEGIC DEFINITION (project requirements)	Estimate time required for Stage 0 services requested, confirm and agree the hourly rate and obtain written instruction from the client to proceed.
1 PREPARATION AND BRIEF	Client to confirm architect's appointment at Stage 1 and contract to be signed by client and architect.
	Time charge for Feasibility Studies provided at Stage 1.
	Agree number of hours in advance. If more time is necessary, seek agreement in advance.
	File the client agreement(s) with the original appointment contract.
2 CONCEPT DESIGN	Obtain client's written agreement to any change in brief or increase in the budget during Stage 2.
	File the client agreement with the original appointment contract.
	For any additional services at Stage 2, email the client with an estimate of the time required and request written agreement(s) to proceed.
	File the client agreement(s) with the original appointment contract.
3 DEVELOPED DESIGN	As Stage 2.
4 TECHNICAL DESIGN	As Stage 2. In addition:
	Prepare pre-tender estimate and, if over budget, seek client agreement to proceed.
	If tenders come back over budget and the additional cost is agreed with the client, file the client's written agreement with the original appointment contract. Also, do this if the client's brief is revised to bring the cost down.
5 CONSTRUCTION	During construction keep the client informed of the estimated final account figure and record any changes to the original brief or cost increase. Request written agreement from the client.
	For any additional services email the client with an estimate of the time required and seek agreement to proceed.
	File the client agreement(s) with the original appointment contract.
6 HANDOVER AND CLOSE OUT (post-Practical Completion)	Check that final account is in line with the approved budget. Obtain written approval of the completed construction and the final account before submitting a Stage 6 invoice.
	File the client agreement(s) with the original appointment contract.
7 IN USE (post-contract)	Time-charge if any services are required. Estimate time required and confirm hourly rate, and seek written agreement to proceed.

Summary

- Make sure the client has understood the contract terms, in particular the terms relating to disputes and professional indemnity.

- Make sure the client is aware of duties under the CDM Regulations.

- Before doing any work on a new project obtain written agreement to your terms, whether this is a few hours' work on an hourly charge basis or a signed appointment contract for the project.

- Keep your client informed of any change to brief/budget or programme at all stages of the project.

- Obtain written agreement from the client to any increase in budget or change to the brief or programme at any stage of the project.

- File with the original appointment contract all the correspondence from the client authorising any increase to the budget or change to the brief.

CDM: Construction (Design and Management) Regulations 2015

The CDM Regulations were introduced more than twenty years ago to improve the health and safety of operatives on site during construction and when carrying out maintenance on buildings, and to ensure that buildings were designed in such a way as to make it safe to build and maintain them. If an accident happens, the current CDM Regulations ensure that there will be a duty holder who can be held accountable, and a paper trail showing what risks were identified and what preventative measures were taken.

The Regulations apply to all construction projects where one or more designers and one or more contractors are appointed. For very small projects where no designer is appointed and there is only one contractor, the CDM Regulations do not apply.

The duties of the various parties under the CDM Regulations 2015 are dealt with differently on a domestic project than on a commercial project. These duties are summarised in the table below. It is only since 2015 that domestic clients have had any duties – before that they were exempt. The domestic client must appoint a principal designer and a principal contractor, but the other client duties are passed to the principal contractor or, subject to written agreement, to the principal designer.

If the domestic client fails to appoint a principal designer or a principal contractor, the designer in control of the design will be the principal designer and the contractor in control of the construction work will be the principal contractor and will also take on the client duties.

Roles and duties on domestic projects

ROLE	MAIN DUTIES

DOMESTIC CLIENT	• Appoint a designer at pre-construction stage as 'principal designer'.
	• Appoint a contractor as 'principal contractor' for the construction phase (if more than one contractor will be on site).
	• Ensure that welfare facilities are provided.
	• Hand over any existing information relating to health and safety.
	• Make suitable arrangements for managing the project.
	• Review arrangements during the project.
	• Provide information about the site.
	• Allow sufficient time and resources for the project.
	• Establish a single point of contact.
	• Arrange for the project to be notified to the Health and Safety Executive (if the project is notifiable).
	• Ensure that the following documents are prepared:
	  • Pre-construction information
	  • Construction Phase Plan
	  • Health and Safety File.
	• Pass some domestic client duties to other duty holders:
	  • To the principal contractor during the construction phase (default), or;
	  • To the principal designer for the pre-construction and construction phases, subject to written agreement.

PRINCIPAL DESIGNER	• Carry out principal designer duties.
	• Subject to appointment carry out domestic client duties as well as principal designer duties during the pre-construction and construction phases.
	• Prepare the pre construction information.
	• Ensure the construction phase plan is produced by the principal contractor prior to construction.
	• Develop the Health and Safety File and provide relevant information to the principal contractor during construction.
	• Hand over the Health and Safety File to the client at practical completion.
PRINCIPAL CONTRACTOR	• Liaise with the principal designer, other contractors and the client.
	• Prepare the Construction Phase Plan.
	• Plan, manage and monitor the construction phase.
	• Ensure the following:
	• site inductions are given to workers
	• steps are taken to prevent unauthorised access to the site
	• provision of welfare facilities.
	• Provide information for the Health and Safety File.
	• Prepare and hand over the Health and Safety File if no principal designer is appointed during the construction phase.
DESIGNER(S)	• Design out or manage risk with regard to health and safety.
	• Liaise with the principal designer.
	• Provide information for the pre-construction information.
CONTRACTOR(S)	• Plan, manage, monitor construction work so it is carried out safely.
	• Liaise with the principal contractor.
	• Provide information for the Construction Phase Plan.
WORKER(S)	• Must be consulted about matters that affect their health and safety.
	• Take care of their own health and safety.
	• Report anything that might affect health and safety.
	• Cooperate with employer, fellow workers, contractors and other duty holders.

Note: Domestic client duties will be taken over by the principal contractor during construction if the principal designer is not appointed for the construction phase of the project.

The regulations can be read in full online.[17] Guidance to the CDM Regulations is also available online.[18]

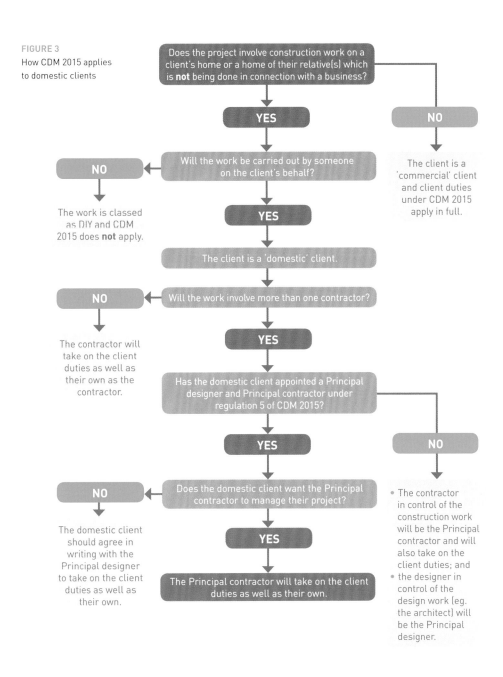

FIGURE 3
How CDM 2015 applies
to domestic clients

CDM: Principal designer and other appointments

Principal designer

On small and domestic projects the architect will nearly always be appointed as the 'principal designer' as defined in the CDM Regulations 2015 (see page 140). You may also assume responsibility for domestic client duties. You should check with your professional indemnity insurers that you are covered to provide this service, as it is completely separate from the services you provide as an architect.

If you are appointed as 'principal designer', this role should be noted in your appointment with an explanation of the work you will do and an estimate of how many hours are required at the different stages. A separate fee for this service should be agreed.

Your clients may not be aware of the CDM Regulations, so you must explain the duties and further clarify that, subject to written agreement, you will be taking over the domestic client duties under the Regulations and providing principal designer services up to Practical Completion.

Other designers

It will be the responsibility of the principal designer to coordinate other designers working on the project and ensure that their designs also comply with the Regulations. Other designers might include specialist glaziers, kitchen designers, mechanical engineers or plumbers.

Principal contractor

On small projects the main contractor will be named as the principal contractor in the construction contract. It will then be the main contractor's duty to ensure that subcontractors also comply with the regulations.

CDM Regulations for a domestic project using traditional procurement

RIBA STAGE	ITEM
0 STRATEGIC DEFINITION (PROJECT REQUIREMENTS)	The domestic client is informed of the CDM Regulations 2015 and the duties of all parties, including the duties of the domestic client.
1 PREPARATION AND BRIEF	The domestic client appoints the principal designer.
	The brief is developed and relevant site information is collected.
	The client hands over any relevant health and safety information.
	The client allocates sufficient time and resources to the project.
2 CONCEPT DESIGN	The domestic client appoints the principal designer (if not appointed in Stage 1).
	The domestic client also appoints the principal designer to take on the domestic client duties.
	The principal designer and other designers complete concept design in line with the Regulations: information about the site is collected and health and safety risks are identified, and preventative measures are taken to eliminate or reduce the risks.
3 DEVELOPED DESIGN	Principal and other designers complete the developed design in line with the Regulations. Health and safety risks are identified and preventative measures taken to eliminate or reduce the risks.
4 TECHNICAL DESIGN	Principal designer produces the pre-construction information that will be sent out with the tender documents.
	The pre-construction information contains all relevant details about the project and any significant health and safety risks.
	The main contractor is appointed.
	The principal contractor is appointed.
	The principal contractor produces the Construction Phase Plan before construction commences.
	Construction risks are identified in the Plan and preventative measures are put in place.
	The Health and Safety Executive is notified using form F10 (if the project is notifiable).
	The project is notifiable if work on site is scheduled to: • last longer than 30 working days and with more than 20 workers on site simultaneously, or; • exceeds 500 person days.

RIBA STAGE		ITEM
5	CONSTRUCTION	The principal contractor follows the procedures set out in the Construction Phase Plan on site.
		The Plan is developed during construction.
		The principal designer monitors any design during construction in line with the Regulations.
		The principal contractor provides information for the Health and Safety File during construction.
		As-built drawings are produced by the principal contractor, or latest construction issue* drawings are produced by designers for the Health and Safety File.
		The Health and Safety File is handed to the client.
6	HANDOVER AND CLOSE OUT (post-Practical Completion)	Maintenance after Practical Completion is carried out in accordance with the guidance set out in the Health and Safety File.
		Maintenance is carried out in accordance with the guidance set out in the Health and Safety File.
		Future construction projects use and update the information in the Health and Safety File.
7	IN USE (post-contract)	Maintenance is carried out in accordance with the guidance set out in the Health and Safety File.
		Future construction projects use and update the information in the Health and Safety File.

*Architects may prefer to use the term 'latest construction issue' and avoid using the term 'as-built', because only the contractor knows what has actually been built.

Appointment of other consultants and specialist contractors

Quotes from other consultants

On a small or domestic project it is likely that the client will expect the architect to provide advice on the need for other consultant appointments or specialist companies who provide design or surveying services. Your client will also expect you to decide what consultant services are necessary, to contact the consultants and discuss the brief and their PI insurance cover, and to arrange for a quote for their services. These quotes should be addressed to your client and copied to you so you can confirm that the quote is reasonable. Invoices from consultants should also be addressed to your client and only copied to you if your client wants you to check them before payment is made.

Consultant appointment

It is not a good idea for you as the architect to appoint consultants directly unless this is something you have carefully considered and agreed with your PI insurer. If you are pitching for larger jobs it may be a requirement that you appoint other consultants. This will increase your turnover and perhaps allow the practice to punch above its weight – but there are costs and risks associated with such appointments, and these should be carefully considered.

Occasionally, a domestic client will recommend a consultant engineer or a contractor they have used before. If so, check the consultant or the contractor out in the same way you would check anyone you have not worked with before, by looking at their website, taking up references from other architects or clients, visiting their work and carrying out financial checks.

The consultants and other designers you are likely to work with on small and domestic projects will depend on the complexity and value of the jobs and can include some or all of the following:

- Structural engineer
- Services engineer
- Quantity surveyor
- Interior designer
- Landscape designer
- Party wall surveyor
- CAD survey company
- AV (audio-visual) consultant
- Specialist kitchen supplier
- Specialist roof-light, door, window or glazing company
- Contract designer for mechanical and electrical or furniture design (where the contractor will appoint designers)

If the work you do is consistent in type and value you may find that you can arrange to work with the same consultants, contractors and specialist subcontractors year after year. Not only does this make projects easier to manage, it is a huge benefit to your clients if you can arrange the whole team knowing that you are putting forward experienced consultants and contractors you can vouch for and whose charges are reasonable for the quality of service provided.

Consultant appointments for a small project and traditional procurement

RIBA STAGE	ITEM
0 STRATEGIC DEFINITION (project requirements)	Advise the client on the need for consultants and explain how they can be briefed, selected and appointed.
1 PREPARATION AND BRIEF	Once appointed, the architect may be asked to contact consultants, provide details of the brief and request quotes (for example: CAD survey, structural engineer, quantity surveyor or services engineer).
2 CONCEPT DESIGN	Client appoints main consultants (for example: structural engineer, services engineer or quantity surveyor).
3 DEVELOPED DESIGN	Client may appoint further consultants not appointed at Stage 2 (for example: AV consultant).
4 TECHNICAL DESIGN	Client may appoint further consultants not appointed at Stages 2 –3 (for example: party wall surveyor).
	To meet the programme on small projects specialist contractors with long lead-in periods are often appointed by the client at Stage 4 to carry out design work. For this service a payment can be made that covers design only (for example: fitted kitchen or doors and windows).
5 CONSTRUCTION	Main contractor will appoint consultants or specialist designers if the contract has responsibility for contractor design elements (for example: mechanical and electrical or joinery).
6 HANDOVER AND CLOSE OUT (post-Practical Completion)	N/A
7 IN USE (post-contract)	N/A

Approvals and party wall agreements

Approvals

Even on a small domestic project a number of approvals may be necessary. Establish at Stage 1 which approvals are applicable to the project:

- **PLANNING:**
  - Outline Planning Permission – Stage 1 or 2
  - Lawful Development Certificate (where planning permission is not required but a certificate is required to prove that the development is lawful) – Stage 3
  - Full Planning Permission – Stage 3
  - Listed Building Consent – Stage 3
- **FREEHOLDER:**
  - Freeholder's consent (for projects on leasehold properties) – Stage 2 or 3
- **THAMES WATER:**
  - Build over agreement – for proposals to build over an existing sewer – Stage 4
- **BUILDING CONTROL:**
  - Building Regulations plans approval – Stage 4
  - Building Regulations completion certificate – Stage 5

Planning

Planning applications are normally made online using the Planning Portal[19] at the end of Stage 3.

Prior to making a submission to planning always check the planning website for the local authority and find out whether the proposed development is in a conservation area, whether an existing building is listed, whether the proposed works are permitted development and what restrictions on development are applicable to your application and the planning history for the address.

It is no longer possible to get free pre-application advice from planning over the phone or at the planning office. Pre-applications can be made to check whether the proposal is likely to get planning permission, but the fee is significantly higher than the planning fee and the process can take as long as eight weeks. After the pre-app, a full planning application must be made for a separate fee, and this will take another eight weeks.

Explain the planning process to your clients and show the approval periods on the pre-contract programme. Check with the client whether Stage 4 work should commence before planning permission is granted.

Building Control

Plans approval and site inspections and completion certification can be carried out by the local authority Building Control or by private inspectors, who will notify the local authority of their appointment.

Party wall

Small and domestic projects often require multiple agreements with adjoining owners if works are proposed on or adjacent to the party walls.

In accordance with the Party Wall etc. Act 1996 these agreements with neighbours must be in writing, and the agreement must refer to the relevant section of the Act. Disputes with adjoining owners or failure to reach agreement can cause long delays and disruption, so good early communication and agreement is important. Where appropriate a party wall surveyor should be appointed to deal with all party wall matters, including the serving of notices under the Act, the drawing up of party wall agreements, and the carrying out of condition surveys before and after construction.

In advance of sending out formal notices the client should show the proposals to adjoining owners who are affected, and explain the works. Formal notice under the Act should then be issued. Depending on which section of the Act applies, one or two months' notice must be given.

The date for issue of notices and the period of notice should be shown on the pre-contract programme.

Sustainability

Due to worldwide concern over climate change our awareness of the importance of 'sustainability' has increased. Countries around the world are working together, recognising that unless all countries cooperate a global solution will not be found.

Along with 180 countries the UK signed up to the Kyoto Protocol in 1995, but the United States and China did not ratify the protocol – so while some progress in the right direction was made, the targets were not met.

- The **Kyoto Protocol** is an international treaty set up to obligate State Parties to collectively reduce greenhouse gas emissions, based on the fact that global warming exists and human-made CO_2 emissions are the sole cause. The Kyoto Protocol is named after Kyoto, Japan, where it was implemented on 11 December 1997. The protocol requires developed countries to reduce their current emissions on the basis that they are historically responsible for the current levels of greenhouse gases in the atmosphere.
- The **Climate Change Act 2008** commits the UK to reducing emissions by at least 80% in 2050 from 1990 levels. This is an enormous challenge and will require a major change to the way we build, live and travel – but then 2050 is a long way off.
- The **Green Deal** was launched by the UK government in 2013 to promote improvements to the existing housing stock – but it did not offer good value, had little take-up and funding has now been stopped.
- The **Paris Climate Conference** in December 2015 led to the first adoption of a universal global climate deal. 195 countries agreed to the plan to avoid dangerous climate change by limiting global warming to well below 2°C.

The UK's decision in June 2016 to exit the European Union has not yet (by the time of writing) had any effect on legislation relating to climate change and carbon reduction.

The **Building Regulations** in the UK, despite the regular updates to Part L in particular, only go some of the way to meet the targets for reduced consumption of energy and carbon emissions that the UK has agreed to meet.

Refurbishment of existing buildings

In facing the challenge to reduce UK energy consumption and carbon emissions associated with the built environment architects must accept that we are not starting from scratch with a programme to build new zero or low carbon buildings on green field sites. The reality is that our cities throughout the UK, especially London, are already built up with millions of existing buildings and a huge amount of work needs to be done to improve the existing buildings especially the housing stock as much of it is over a hundred years old. Reducing energy consumption from the existing housing stock is a major challenge and calls for innovative technical solutions, long-term strategies and tax incentives, achievable targets and proper funding at government level.

Many small architectural practices and sole practitioners work on existing buildings throughout the UK repairing the existing fabric of buildings, improving the thermal performance and reducing the consumption of energy, and giving old buildings a new lease of life. Refurbishment work does not have the eco glamour of large newbuild low carbon projects that use innovative technology, but refurbishment has a small carbon footprint compared to new build and is important if we are to achieve the target reduction in UK carbon emissions.

Client commitment to sustainability

Some clients are passionate about energy-saving technology and measures; others show little or no interest. It will be up to you as the architect to provide the information clients need to make informed decisions about appropriate measures for their particular project and budget. You might find it useful to have a checklist in the office manual of all the energy-saving measures that can be considered, from loft insulation to wind turbines, and a list of items to check on site that can have an impact on sustainability. Keep your client informed at all stages about the costs and benefits of the energy-saving measures included in the project, and be aware that if savings need to be made these items may be the first to go if the client does not understand the real benefit.

Designing buildings with low embodied energy and a small carbon footprint that reduce fossil fuel use can add to the work required to detail, specify and construct the building. Your fee should reflect this extra work, and any additional construction cost should be offset against future savings. This aspect should be discussed with clients.

Sustainability checklist for a small project with traditional procurement

RIBA STAGE		SUSTAINABILITY CHECKLIST
0	STRATEGIC DEFINITION (project requirements)	Discuss and establish broad aims for sustainability with the client.
1	PREPARATION AND BRIEF	Discuss with the client what improvements or thermal values are mandatory under the Building Regulations, and what additional improvements or new construction can be considered to reduce future energy consumption. Discuss the financial implications, including spending more now to save on bills in the future, and mention that some equipment that harnesses energy also requires maintenance and may be obsolete before the cost has been recuperated through reduced bills. Make suggestions about how energy consumption can be reduced.
		If instructed by your client, carry out feasibility studies or cost comparisons using different energy-saving measures.
		Confirm the client's brief in relation to sustainability and include the cost in the Stage 1 budget.
2	CONCEPT DESIGN	Incorporate into the brief and concept design proposals the energy-saving measures you have agreed with your client.
		Include the cost in the Stage 2 budget.
3	DEVELOPED DESIGN	Produce and develop a design incorporating the agreed energy-saving measures. Obtain client agreement to the proposals
		Include the cost in the Stage 3 budget.
4	TECHNICAL DESIGN	Develop the energy-saving measures agreed in Stage 3. Obtain quotes where applicable.
		Obtain client agreement to the proposals.
		Include the cost in the pre-tender estimate.
		If tenders come back over budget and savings must be made, review the whole project with the client and try to avoid omitting the specified energy-saving measures, as this is sometimes seen as an easy way to make savings.
		The cost is now in the agreed contract sum in the contract.
5	CONSTRUCTION	Ensure that the sustainability strategy for the project and the energy-saving measures specified are carried through into construction.
		Hand over the building to the client, together with the Health and Safety File and relevant manuals and guarantees so the building can be used and maintained and the performance monitored by the client as intended.
6	HANDOVER AND CLOSE OUT (post-Practical Completion)	Monitor performance of equipment and as-built construction during the defects liability period and get feedback from the client on comfort, performance and reduced bills.
7	IN USE (post-contract)	You will rarely be appointed to provide services at Stage 7 on a small or domestic project, but you should be able to carry out a simple post-occupancy evaluation of the systems installed at the end of the defects liability period.
		The client should be able to monitor the performance of the building post-contract.

Pre-contract programme and construction programme

A pre-contract programme sets out all the key stages of the project and can be prepared and issued to the client at Stage 1, as soon as the brief has been confirmed. The programme should then be revised and reissued at each stage of the project. You can also show on the programme the stages at which you will invoice the client and approximate dates for valuations when the project is on site. Domestic clients often need to carefully manage cashflow and move money between accounts to have money ready to pay invoices. The more warning you give them of when payments are due the better prepared they will be to make prompt payment to you, the other consultants and the contractor.

See Figure 4 Pre-contract programme overleaf.

Construction programme

A construction programme should be provided by the contractor at the pre-contract meeting, and it should show all the key stages of the construction on site. The programme should also show periods for drawing approvals and latest dates for long-order items and long manufacture periods, as delivery periods for items such as doors and windows can be up to sixteen weeks. In some cases orders may need to be placed with specialist suppliers or subcontractors prior to the appointment of the main contractor. If there are delays on the project the programme should be updated by the contractor and issued with any request for an extension of time. A valuation forecast can also be added to the programme by the contractor. This will help clients have money ready to pay when interim certificates are issued. It is also helpful to monitor progress on site.

See Figure 5 Construction programme on page 158.

ABC ARCHITECTS
PRE CONTRACT PROGRAMME (TRADITIONAL PROCUREMENT)
PROJECT ADDRESS:
Ref:
Date

		2017																				
	WORK STAGE	January					February				March				April				May			
RIBA STAGE	Week commencing Monday	2	9	16	23	30	6	13	20	27	6	13	20	27	3	10	17	24	1	8	15	22
	Pre appointment discussion																					
1	Confirmation of arch appointment	X																				
1	Confirmation of client brief / budget																					
1	Dimension survey																					
1,2	Scheme design and budget																					
3	Developed design + budget																					
3	Planning application Listed building consent							X														
4	Detail design																					
4	Construction drawings																					
4	Structural design																					
4	Appoint building inspector Building regs plans approval														X							
4	NBS specification / tender document																					
4	Tender																					
4	Tender consideration and appointment Pre contract meeting																					
4	Surveyor appointment Party wall awards in place														X							
5	Lead in & pre contract meeting																					
5,6	Construction																					
6	End of defects laibility period																					
5,6	Valuations																					
1-6	Architect site visits	X		X			X						X									
1-6	Architect fee invoices approx issue		1	2			3											4				5

FIGURE 4.
Pre-contract programme

		July						August				September				October					November				December				January					March		
																																		2018			
12	19	26	3	10	17	24	31	7	14	21	28	4	11	18	25	2	9	16	23	30	6	13	20	27	4	11	18	25	1	8	15	22	29			
X																																				
																																		X		
	1				2				3				4																							5
X	X	X	X	X	X	X	X	X	X	X	X	X	X	X																			X	X	
	6				7				8				9																							

FIGURE 5
Construction programme

MAIN CONTRACTOR NAME
CONSTRUCTION PROGRAMME
PROJECT ADDRESS:
Ref:
Date

	2017																							DEFECTS PERIOD
WORK STAGE	January					February				March				April				May						October
Week commencing Monday	2	9	16	23	30	6	13	20	27	6	13	20	27	3	10	17	24	1	8	15	22	29		
Week No	1	2	3	4	5	6	7	8	9	10	11	12	13	14										
Valuations		1					2				3				4									5
Cash Flow Forecast		£15,000 + vat					£65,000 + vat				£65,000 + vat				£45,000 + vat									release of 2.5% retention
Overall Programme																								defects
Site Set Up site office, welfare, secure storage, hoardings etc																								
Asbestos survey																								
Internal Strip Out																								
Drainage Survey																								
Demolition and alterations																								
Foundations																								
Structural works																								
Extension External walls																								
Extension roof																								
Specialist subcontractor: Sarna roof	x	lead in				on	site																	
Floors																								
Internal walls and partitions																								
Drainage above and below ground																								
1st fix carpenter																								
1st fix electrician																								
1st fix plumber																								
specialist subcontractor: aluminium doors + r'light	x	dwgs & manufacture					on	site																
specialist subcontractor: new timber windows	x	dwgs & manufacture					on	site																
Plaster walls and ceiling																								
2nd fix carpenter																								
2nd fix electrician																								
2nd fix plumber																								
Wall tiling																								
Sanitary ware																								
Specialist kitchen subcontractor – Kitchen	x	dwgs & manufacture					on	site																
worktop splashback										worktops														
Fixtures and fittings																								
External works																								
Decorations																								
Floor finishes																								
Clean and handover / snagging																								

Programmes for a small project with traditional procurement

RIBA STAGE		PROGRAMME
0	STRATEGIC DEFINITION (project requirements)	Client/Architect discussion about the programme
1	PREPARATION AND BRIEF	Pre-contract programme – prepared by the architect
2	CONCEPT DESIGN	Pre-contract programme updated
3	DEVELOPED DESIGN	Pre-contract programme updated
4	TECHNICAL DESIGN	Pre-contract programme updated Construction programme issued by the contractor
5	CONSTRUCTION	Construction programme updated by the contractor
6	HANDOVER AND CLOSE OUT (post-Practical Completion)	Construction programme updated by the contractor
7	IN USE (post-contract)	N/A

Drawings and drawing issue sheet

Drawings

The project drawings will normally include:

- general arrangement drawings
- assembly drawings
- detail drawings.

The title block on the drawings will include:

- practice name
- contact details
- project title
- drawing title
- drawing number
- date of drawing
- revision number
- drawing author
- scale
- north point
- key to symbols.

In addition, the title block may contain a copyright symbol and an instruction not to scale from the drawing.

For new buildings, the architect will set up the drawings from scratch. For works to existing buildings, a full CAD survey with levels should be commissioned. This survey should highlight walls that are not plumb and floors that are not level, as well as if the building is not orthogonal.

Domestic clients and other inexperienced clients are likely to change their minds throughout the design process and will often want to wait until the last minute to select finishes or furniture layouts, so be clear about what information you need to show on drawings at each stage of the design and show no more than this. Remember that the more lines and objects there are on a drawing or schedule, the longer it will take to revise. If you show the same information on three different drawings, all three may have to be revised. Try to get final decisions from your client as soon as possible in the design process, and remember to update the programme and the budget at each stage and obtain agreement to any increase in cost or delay to the programme.

Traditional procurement is still widely used for small projects and domestic projects. This means that the design, or most of it, will be complete before tenders are obtained at Stage 4. The design and detail will be developed during Stages 1, 2, 3, 4 and 5 in accordance with the RIBA Plan of Work as shown below.

Drawings for a small project using traditional procurement

RIBA STAGE	ITEM
0 PROJECT REQUIREMENTS	N/A
1 STRATEGIC DEFINITION (project requirements)	Drawings at the end of Stage 1 should show completed feasibility studies and sufficient information for the client to confirm the project brief and to obtain client agreement to proceed to Stage 2. On refurbishment projects, arrange for a measured CAD survey with levels.
2 CONCEPT DESIGN	Concept design drawings at the end of Stage 2 should show sufficient information to explain the proposals and to obtain client agreement to proceed to Stage 3. Drawings (sufficiently detailed to explain the design): 1:250 Location plan 1:500 Site plan 1:100 Plans, sections, elevations
3 DEVELOPED DESIGN	Developed design drawings at the end of Stage 3 should show sufficient information to apply for planning approval and (if applicable) listed building consent, and to obtain client agreement to proceed to Stage 4. Drawings (sufficiently detailed for planning submission): 1:250 Location plan 1:500 Site plan 1:100 or 1:50 Plans, sections, elevations
4 TECHNICAL DESIGN	Drawings at the end of Stage 4 should show sufficient detailed information to obtain tenders, to obtain Building Regulations plans approval and for construction, and to obtain client agreement to go out to tender. If tender drawings are not sufficiently detailed for construction then further detail should be added before the drawings are issued for construction. Drawings should be issued with a drawing issue sheet and the issue confirmed by instruction. Any revisions on construction issue drawings should have revision clouds, as the revisions must be measured and priced by the contractor. Drawings (sufficiently detailed for pricing): 1:100 Site plan showing drainage 1:50 Plans, sections, elevations 1:20 Detailed plans, sections 1:10, 1:5 Detail schedules

RIBA STAGE	ITEM
5 CONSTRUCTION	Drawings issued during Stage 5 are issued for construction. These drawings will be prepared by the architect or by the contractor (where there is a contractor design element within the contract, for example the mechanical and electrical design on a domestic project).
	At Practical Completion a set of latest construction issue drawings will be prepared by the architect and issued to the client. The contractor will issue as-built drawings for contractor design elements.
	Drawings (sufficiently detailed for construction): 1:100 Site plan showing drainage 1:50 Plans, sections, elevations 1:20 Detailed plans, sections 1:10, 1:5 Detail schedules
6 HANDOVER	N/A
7 IN USE (post Practical Completion)	N/A

Depending on the size and complexity of the project there may be more than one drawing issue at each stage.

A3/PDF drawings

Many small architectural practices only have A3 printers. On small jobs both architects and contractors may prefer to use A3 drawings and PDFs, as they can easily be printed in-house and in the domestic client's house or the small contractor's office. A3 drawings can be bound into an A4 tender document and kept in an A3 file on site, and revised drawings added to the file as they are issued. A3 drawings are also easy to archive.

Increasingly, small contractors are using digital devices including mobile phones to look at PDFs of drawings and specifications. The danger of looking at a large drawing on a small digital device is that the whole drawing or document is not seen and not all the operatives on site will have access to the device with the information. You should insist that an up-to-date hard copy of the current drawings and the specification are on site in one place and kept up to date throughout the construction period, and accessible to the operatives carrying out the work. If it is written into the preliminaries the contractor must comply with the requirement.

The text on drawings should be big enough to be clearly legible, and preferably black on white. It is not enough that the architect can clearly see what is written on the drawings. The client or contractor, possibly with poor eyesight, should also be able to read the drawings with relative ease. Remember that the lighting on site is not always as good as it is in the office.

Drawing issue sheet

Every issue of drawings to your client at the pre-contract stage should be recorded on a drawing issue sheet such as the example shown in Figure 6. The same sheet should be used for going out to tender, and any further drawings issued during construction should be recorded on the drawing issue sheet and the issue confirmed by a site/architect's instruction. At Practical Completion the drawing issue sheet will show all the drawings issued during the project, the date they were issued, to whom they were issued and for what purpose. A copy of the drawing issue sheet can be included in the Health and Safety File/Building Manual handed over to the client.

ABC ARCHITECTS

DRAWING ISSUE SHEET

ADDRESS.......

JOB NO.......

DRAWINGS

SIZE	SCALE	DRAWING TITLE	NUMBER	4.8.2015	11.8.2015	29.8.2015	14.9.2015	24.9.2015	4.11.2015	30.11.2015 (tender)	1.12.2015
A4	1:1250	OS MAP	1508 OS	X							
A3	1:100	Site Plan And First Floor Plan - Demolition	1508 D1	X		X	X	X		X	
A3	1:100	Second Floor Plan And Loft Floor Plan - Demolition	1508 D2	X		X	X			X	
A3	1:100	Elevations - Demolition	1508 D3	X		X	X	X		X	
A3	1:100	Section A-A - Demolition	1508 D4	X		X	X	X		X	
A3	1:100	Boundary 7,9 Berriman Rd	1508 E5							2	
A3	1:100	Site Plan - Proposed	1508 WD0	1	2	3	4	4		6	6
A3	1:50	Ground Floor Plan - Proposed	1508 WD1	1	2	3	4	4	4A	6	6
A3	1:50	First Floor Plan - Proposed	1508 WD2	1	2	3	4	4	4A	6	6
A3	1:50	Second Floor Plan - Proposed	1508 WD3	1	2	3	4	4	4A	6	6
A3	1:50	Loft Plan - Proposed	1508 WD4	1	2	3	4	4	4A	6	6
A3	1:50	Roof Plan - Proposed	1508 WD5	1	2	3	4	4	4A	6	6
A3	1:50	Front Elevation - Proposed	1508 WD6	1	2	3	4	4	4A	6	6
A3	1:50	Rear Elevation - Proposed	1508 WD7	1	2	3	4	4	4A	6	6
A3	1:50	Section A-A Proposed	1508 WD8	1	2	3	4	4	4A	6	6
A3	1:50	Section B-B, C-C Proposed	1508 WD9				4	4	4A	SUPERSEDED	
A3	1:50	Kitchen Dining	1508 WD10							6	6

DATE OF ISSUE

FIGURE 6.

Drawing issue register

Drawing Schedule

Size	Scale	Title	Drawing No.	Copies	Copies
A3	—	Elevations			
A3	1:50	New Doors, Windows, Rooflights	1508 WD12	6	6
A3	1:25	Extension - Section E-E	1508 WD20	6	6
A3	1:25	Extension - Section F-F	1508 WD21	6	6
A3	1:25	Extension Sections B-B, C-C	1508 WD22	6	6
A3	1:25	Built In Bookcase	1508 WD23	6	6
A3	1:25	Construction Details	1508 WD25	6	6
A3	1:25	New Timber Deck	1508 WD30	6	6
A3	N/A	Schedule 1 - Finishes	1508 SCH1	6	
A3	N/A	Schedule 2 - Sanitary Fittings	1508 SCH 2	6	
A3	N/A	Schedule 3 - Light Fittings	1508 SCH 3	6	6
A3	N/A	Schedule 4 - Kitchen Fittings And Appliances	1508 SCH 4	6	
A3	1:50@A1	Structural Proposals	7491-1A REV 1	Rev 1	Rev 2

NUMBER OF COPIES ISSUED

DISTRIBUTION												
CLIENT	X	X	X	X	X	X	X	X			X	
FILE	X	X	X	X	X	X	X	X			X	
PLANNING			X	X	X							
BUILDING CONTROL											X	
CONTRACTOR												
M+E CONSULTANT												X

PURPOSE OF ISSUE

COMMENTS												
INFORMATION	X											
APPROVAL	X	X	X	X				X			X	
COSTING											X	
TENDER											X	
CONSTRUCTION												
PARTY WALL AGREEMENTS												X

Specification and cost control

Specification

The outline specification will be developed from a broad list of headings at Stage 1 to a more detailed description of the project at Stage 3.

At Stage 4 a fully detailed specification is written using a standard format such as:

- NBS Minor Works Specification
- NBS Intermediate Specification
- NBS Domestic Specification (priced per copy and only suitable for small domestic projects).

NBS Minor Works and NBS Intermediate software is licensed and regularly updated to be compatible with the latest version of the construction contracts. Most good small contractors are familiar with the NBS.

The NBS specification and preliminaries will be included in the tender documents sent out to tender and used by the contractors to price the tender. The work sections in the NBS specification are set out in alphabetical order and in the same sequence as construction:

C – Demolition

D – Groundworks

E – Concrete

F – Masonry etc.

Most of the work should be fully specified but there may be some items that will be performance or part-performance specified such as mechanical and electrical work. If any part of the work is performance specified you must use a construction contract with provision for contractor design such as JCT Minor Works with Contractor Design or the RIBA Domestic or Concise building contracts.

In order for tender pricing to be accurate the drawings and specifications sent out to tender should describe and specify the works in detail. If the tender documents are not fully detailed and include too many large provisional sums there is a risk that the cost of the project will increase during construction.

Cost control

At each stage of the project the specification and the budget should become more detailed. When you prepare a budget you should know where your figures come from. This might be from a pricing book, a quote from a supplier or contractor, a £/m² rate based on a similar job recently tendered, or by estimating how long work will take and using day rates for the different trades. A budget for a small newbuild project could be set out as follows:

CLIENT APPROVAL OF THE DRAWINGS, SPECIFICATION AND BUDGET SHOULD BE OBTAINED AT THE END OF EACH STAGE BEFORE PROCEEDING TO THE NEXT STAGE.

Construction cost budget

STAGE (1, 2 OR 3) CONSTRUCTION COST BUDGET			
PROJECT: (ADDRESS)			
HEADING	QUANTITY	£/M²	TOTAL
Substructure • superstructure • external walls • ground floor • upper floors • internal walls • windows • doors • roof.			
Internal finishes			
Fittings			
Services			
Drainage			
External works			
Prelims			
Temporary works			
Contingency			
Other			
Total construction cost			

This budget excludes fees and other expenses.

Budgets for refurbishment work will include VAT and the format will depend on the scope of the work. Contractors pricing a refurbishment tender often estimate the cost of small quantities of work on the length of time the work will take and the cost of materials, rather than using a £/m^2 rate.

When calculating the fee on a small project where a quantity surveyor is not appointed, you must ensure that your fee covers the time you will spend preparing pre-contract budgets, sending out tenders, analysing tenders and agreeing the cost of variations, interim valuations and the final account.

Quantity surveyor advice

It is unlikely that a quantity surveyor will be appointed if the contract value is less than £250,000, so you must write and develop the specification and produce the budgets at Stages 1, 2 and 3. It is important to get the budget right at the earliest stage of the project, otherwise your client could hold you responsible for incorrect advice or for the project going over-budget in the later stages. If you do not have the expertise to produce an accurate budget you must arrange for a quantity surveyor to be appointed, even if on an hourly charge basis for a few hours.

If the project budget is over £250,000, or if the construction is particularly complicated, a quantity surveyor should be appointed. The quantity surveyor will update the budgets from your specification and drawings at each key stages of the project. If appointed for the whole project the quantity surveyor will also prepare a pre-tender estimate and analyse the tenders. Once the project is on site they will agree the cost of variations with the contractor, interim valuations and the final account.

Contingency

A contingency figure should be included in the early stage budgets and the contract sum to allow for the cost of additional work that invariably has to be instructed on site but cannot be foreseen at design stage. Otherwise, you must obtain client consent for the additional cost every time an instruction is issued that has a cost implication.

Specification and budget for a small project with traditional procurement

RIBA STAGE		SPECIFICATION AND BUDGET
0	STRATEGIC DEFINITION (project requirements)	The specification at this stage will be no more than a short description of the project requirements and a budget based on approximate area and average £/m2 for the type of building proposed plus fees. Inform your client about the 20% VAT on refurbishment contracts and on consultants' fees.
		At the end of this stage confirm the client requirements before proceeding to Stage 1.
1	PREPARATION AND BRIEF	The specification at the end of this stage will be an outline spec with broad descriptions and approximate areas against which you will be able to put a budget cost. For example, preliminaries might be 15% and an extension might be 20m2 and costed at £2,500/m2, or a kitchen fitout at £30k.
		Obtain client approval for the brief and budget before proceeding to Stage 2.
2	CONCEPT DESIGN	The specification at this stage will still be an outline spec, but in more detail than Stage 1. You may have decided that the extension will now be 25m2 and built in brick with a flat roof and electrically operated roof lights and aluminium sliding doors, so these elements can be measured and budgeted more accurately than at Stage 1.
		Obtain client approval to the outline specification and budget before proceeding to Stage 3.
3	DEVELOPED DESIGN	The specification at this stage will describe the project accurately, with a full description of all the materials selected and provisional sums to cover elements not yet selected or fully detailed. You may have decided that the extension will have a hardwood floor but you have not selected a flooring product so you will include a provisional £/m2 to cover the flooring, underlay and labour. Another provisional sum might cover the extra cost of underfloor heating instead of radiators. This decision might be subject to budget. You may also have obtained quotes for specialist items such as a fitted kitchen, windows, doors, glazing or sanitary fittings.
		Obtain client approval to the developed specification and budget before proceeding to Stage 4.

RIBA STAGE		SPECIFICATION AND BUDGET
4	TECHNICAL DESIGN	The specification at this stage will be fully detailed using the NBS Minor Works Specification or NBS Intermediate, or a similar standard specification document. The tender document will include a full set of preliminaries and construction clauses so every element of the contract is specified and priced by the contractor.
		A pre-tender estimate should be issued to the client for approval before going out to tender.
		When tenders are returned, if the project is over-budget it may be necessary to go through an exercise to reduce the specification to bring the scheme back within budget.
		Obtain client approval to any revisions to the specification and the cost before the client signs the contract with the contractor and before proceeding to Stage 5.
5	CONSTRUCTION	Any variations to the works during construction should be confirmed with a site instruction.
		Obtain client approval to any change in the specification and the estimated final contract value before issue of site instructions.
		At each valuation check the estimated final account and agree the account with the client. Consultants' fees and any other fees, as well as VAT should be added to the estimate.
		Before granting Practical Completion obtain agreement from your client that the works and the current estimate of the final account are satisfactory.
6	HANDOVER AND CLOSE OUT (post-Practical Completion)	The final account at this stage should not come as a surprise to the client if estimated final accounts have been agreed up to the last valuation.
		Agree the final account including VAT with the contractor and the client.
		Agree other final costs with the client including fees, expenses and VAT.
		If you are using a JCT contract remind your client that 2.5% will be held back and paid to the contractor at the end of the defects liability period.
7	STRATEGIC DEFINITION (project requirements)	N/A

Selecting a contractor

Traditional procurement

For small and domestic projects traditional procurement is still widely used. This means the project is tendered at Stage 4 of the Plan of Work, when the design is complete. If there is a contractor design element in the contract this element of the design will be completed in Stage 5 during construction. The advantage of traditional procurement for domestic clients in particular is the knowledge that the scheme has been fully designed and priced competitively before the client signs a contract with a contractor.

Tender list

For contracts above £50,000 and below £1,000,000 it is common to have three or four contractors on a tender list. Fewer than this can be problematic if one or two drop out during the tender period, or fail to submit a tender. More than this and the good contractors will lose interest, as their chance of getting the job is reduced. The cost for a contractor of pricing a tender is significant, even if the project is relatively small such as a refurbishment or extension of a domestic property, so the tendering contractors want to know they have a reasonable chance of winning the tender.

Contractor selection

You should have a long list of contractors in the office. Before you go out to tender at Stage 4 make sure that every contractor on the tender list is properly checked out (and that the checks are up to date) and that each contractor is one you would be happy to recommend to your client. Remember that a contractor who is ideal for one client might not be right for another client.

Always choose contractors who have the same attitude towards their work as you do. Otherwise, no matter how hard you work or how many drawings are produced, how many phone calls you make or how many extra site visits you carry out, the finished work will not meet your standards.

If a competent and experienced contractor is appointed, the quality of the completed work on site will be good and it will be relatively easy and enjoyable to administer the contract. Your client will be more relaxed during the construction and pleased with the end result. You are likely to make a decent profit on the project and you may even learn from the contractor. If on the other hand a contractor is appointed who is not quite up to the job, all parties will struggle the whole way through and the end result will probably be disappointing.

Sometimes a domestic client will want to put a contractor on a tender list because they have done work for a neighbour at a low price. The contractor may well be a good contractor whose prices are reasonable but you should still carry out a financial check and take up a reference, check the contractor's website and if possible visit a job they have done recently. If you find anything untoward this should be discussed openly with your client and if you don't think the contractor is up to the job you should say so. Doing this before a contractor is added to the tender list takes time but may well save time, effort and stress further down the line.

Good small contractors

Good small contractors are like gold dust and are usually busy with work programmed into future months, so always phone to check they are willing to tender and provide details of the project and relevant dates before adding them to the tender list. Confirm their willingness to tender in writing saying when the tenders will go out, and copy in your client so they are included in the process.

Always contact the contractors who have tendered on your projects to thank them for their tender and to let them know whether their tender has been successful. Provide further feedback if requested. Contractors often ask whether the lowest tender figure was selected, what the lowest tender figure was and the basis on which a contractor was selected. The contractors will have spent a significant amount of money pricing your tender and you may want the same contractors to price future tenders, so the simple courtesy of providing feedback is good business.

Tender

Tender documents

For traditional procurement where the contractor is appointed at Stage 4, the tender process is as follows:

- Make a list of three to four contractors based on their suitability for the project.
- Agree the tender list with the client.
- Contact the contractors on the tender list, provide details of the contract and ask the contractors to confirm their willingness to tender.
- Send out the tender documents.
- Check tenders for mistakes or mathematical errors.
- Check contractors' insurance details have been provided.
- Check that contractors can meet the project start and completion dates.
- Send the tender analysis and recommendations to the client for approval.
- Notify the contractor of the client's decision to accept the tender, and arrange a pre-contract meeting where the contract will be signed.
- Notify the other contractors that their tenders have not been successful and provide feedback if requested.

For small projects, and most domestic projects, the documents sent out to tender to the selected list of contractors, with a copy to your client, will include the following:

- letter of invitation to tender (see Figure 8)
- form of tender (see Figure 7)
- preliminaries
- specification
- pricing document or schedule of works
- drawing issue register
- architect's drawings and schedules
- structural engineer's drawings
- site information
- CDM pre-construction information.

FIGURE 7

Tender pricing
document for
a small project
where no QS is
appointed

FORM OF TENDER

For: *(insert description of project)*
At: *(insert address of project)*

We have read the conditions of contract and have examined the specification
and drawings that you have sent us.

We offer to execute and complete in accordance with the conditions of contract
the whole of the works described for the sum of (excluding VAT)

£ ....

(and in words) ....

within *(insert number)* weeks from the date of possession (or alternative
agreed period) of the site.

We enclose a copy of the pricing document giving a breakdown of our
tender figure.

This tender remains open for consideration for one month from the date
fixed for submitting a tender.

Signed and delivered
By the contractor: ....

....

....

....

Date: ....

This tender is to be returned by *(insert time)* p.m. on *(insert date)*
To: ABC Architects Ltd. *(insert address or email address)*

FIGURE 8
Invitation to tender

ABC ARCHITECTS
(Address)
(Email address)

Our ref: *(ref)*
Date: *(date)*
(Address of contractor)

Dear (name),

(Project address)
(Project Description)

Thank you for your confirmation of willingness to tender on this contract.

Please find attached:

- Form of Tender

- Preliminaries, Specification, Drawings and Schedules

- Drawing Issue sheet

- Pricing Document

A digital copy of the tender documents will also be sent to you.

Please return the completed Form of Tender, the pricing document and copies of your insurances to this office by (time and date). The tender may be returned by post or by email to ABC Architects.

Yours Sincerely,

(your name)
For ABC Architects

Cc   *(client name)*

Allow three to four weeks for a single-stage selective tender, as the contractors must ask subcontractors to price part of the works.

Formats for pricing will vary depending on the size and complexity of the project and whether or not a quantity surveyor is appointed. But whatever the size of the project the format used for pricing and analysing tenders, valuations and final accounts should be fit for purpose and efficient to use – and, if possible, consistent from project to project. The document the contractor is asked to price should be set out logically and in the same sequence as the construction on site.

The pricing document will include any provisional sums or prime cost sums (see figure 12).

Provisional sums

A provisional sum is an allowance in the tender document for work that may be necessary but cannot be measured or priced at tender stage. The contractor should include sufficient time in their construction programme to carry out this work. Provisional sums can be 'defined', such as new consumer units (allowed for in the contractor's programme), or 'undefined', such as additional work in connection with services (not allowed for in the contractor's programme).

On refurbishment projects a contingency sum (for example 6% of the construction cost) can be included and will allow for works that may be necessary to build the project but cannot be defined at design stage, such as replacement of rotten timbers or live plaster, or additional work in connection with drainage. If a contingency sum is not included in the contract sum then each additional item instructed on site with a cost implication must be referred to the client for approval.

Prime cost sums

A prime cost sum is an allowance in the tender for work or materials provided by a contractor or supplier named by the client, such as the supply and fitting of an aluminium sliding door. The contractor will add a percentage for profit and attendance.

Pricing document and tender analysis

For a small domestic project a pricing document at tender stage could be a detailed schedule of work or it could be a priced activity schedule like the example in Figure 7, where the tendering contractors will be expected to measure and price the sections of work based on the detailed drawings and NBS Minor Works Specification sent out with the tender. If the project is fully designed and specified in detail the contractors' tenders should include everything, even if the price is not broken down in the same way it would be in a full bill of quantities. If parts of the project are not fully designed, the price for these items can only be provisional and must be priced during construction when details are issued. The same spreadsheet used for the tender can be used for checking and analysing the tenders, as shown in Figure 8.

With traditional procurement, if a project is not fully designed and specified in detail at tender stage and large elements of work are covered by provisional sums, there is a high risk that costs will increase during construction and be more difficult to control. The risk should be explained to your client before going out to tender.

At the same time as checking the figures the contractor's insurances should be checked and the start-on-site date and the contract period confirmed. When you feel confident that you have got the right contractor at the right price, a recommendation can be made to the client.

Contractors can be asked to provide with their tenders day rates for each trade and the percentage that will be added to materials if work is carried out on a day-works basis. This will enable you to control and agree the cost of variations on site. This information can be included in the tender analysis and recommendation to your client.

When analysing a tender on a spreadsheet with three or four columns of figures against the specified work items, it is quite easy to check the maths and see when one contractor has over- or under-priced an item.

If the tenders are all over budget it may be possible to negotiate a reduced scope of works with the input of the client and a preferred contractor to bring the scheme back in line with the budget.

FIGURE 9

Pricing document

NBS CLAUSE	DESCRIPTION	COST SUMMARY £
ABC ARCHITECTS		
PROJECT: (Address)................		
PRICING DOCUMENT		
REF: (Job No) PRICING DOCUMENT		
Date:		
A10-A44	Preliminary Items (contractor to provide breakdown with tender)	
	Provisional Sums	
A54.115	Rebuild garden wall on rear boundary	2,000.00
A54.116	Intruder alarm	600.00
A54.117	Replace kitchen floor screed	500.00
A54.113	Damp and timber treatment	1,000.00
A54.111	Supply of ironmongery	1,400.00
	Prime Cost Sums (Client nominated suppliers and sub contractors)	
A54,309	Supply of sanitary fittings	3,905.50
A54.309	Profit %	
A54.310	Supply and fit sliding doors	6,360.00
A54.310	Profit and attendance %	
A54.311	Supply and fit new timber windows	11,250.00
A54.311	Profit and attendance %	
A54.312	Supply and fit rooflights	6,805.00
A54.312	Profit and attendance %	
A54.590	Contingency	6,500.00
C20	Demolition and strip out	
D20	Excavation	
E10,30,41	Concrete	
F10,31	Brick, block and accessories	
G12	Steel	
G20	Carpentry, timber framing, first fixing	
H71	Lead flashings	
J30	Liquid damp proofing	
J42	Sarna roof with 20 year guarantee	
K10	Gypsum board wall and ceiling lninings	
K11	Ply roof deck, ply flooring	
K21	Oak engineered floor, oak shelves, oak worktop to Living units	
K21	Living: Oak worktop to built in units, WC: oak shelves under basin, oak duct top	
L10	New timber windows (see PC Sum above)	0.00
L10	New rooflights (see PC Sum above)	0.00
L20	New hall door (see PC Sum above)	0.00
L20	Sliding doors (see PC Sum above)	0.00
L20	Internal doors	
L30	Staircase works to balustrade incl oak capping	
L40	Glazing (see PC Sum above)	0.00
M10	Screed	
M20	Plaster, render	
M40	Floor and wall tiling	
M60	Decoration	
N10.11	Purpose made bathroom cabinet	

NBS CLAUSE	DESCRIPTION	COST SUMMARY £
N10.12	Tiled removeable bath panel	
N10.13	Stone top to duct behind WC in bathroom	
N10.14	TV and lighting recesses on living room wall	
N10.16	Pull out laundry box	
N10.86	Fireplace cladding to sides and front removeable panel	
N11.9	Fitted kitchen – CLIENT DIRECT ORDER	0.00
N11.9	Attendance by main contractor incl mechanical and electric	
N13.9	Fix only sanitary fittings, accessories and heated towel rail (supply covered by PC Sum above)	
P10	Insulation not priced elsewhere	
P20	Skirtings, architraves, mirrors	
P21	Fix only ironmongery incl in L10, L20 (supply covered by PC Sum above)	0.00
P30,31	Builders' work in connection with services	
Q20,25	Stone paving and sub base	
Q28	Topsoil	
Q40	Rear garden: New 1.5m fence and gate to No6/No7 and No6/public footpath	
R10	Rainwater drainage	
R11	Foul drainage above ground	
R12	Drainage below ground	
S90	Hot and cold water supplies	
S91	Gas	
T90	Heating	
U90	Mechanical extract and duct to kitchen and bathroom	
V90	Electrical	
V90	Supply of light fittings and bulbs	
W90	TV, smoke alarm	
Z10-22	Workmanship clauses	0.00
	The contractor to price here for any items shown on the drawings or included in the specification or deemed necessary and not included above	
	Sub total	
	VAT	
	Total	
	Contractor to price here for rates to be used in Pricing of Variations and /or expenditure of provisional Sums	
	Daywork rates for trades:	£
	Plumber	
	Electrician	
	Carpenter	
	Bricklayer	
	Plasterer	
	Tiler	
	Decorator	
	Labourer	
	Variations: % mark up on materials	%

What might at first glance appear to be the lowest tender may not be the best tender to choose, so check all the figures and anything that might cause a problem during construction. Watch out for the following in tenders from small contractors:

- Front-loaded costs mean the contractor gets more cash in the early stages of the job. The danger is that if the contractor goes under, there will not be enough money to get another contractor to complete the project. It is also possible that the contractor will experience cashflow problems towards the end of the job.
- Relatively high contractor's preliminaries and relatively low costs against the specified work items mean that early valuations could be too high and variations will be expensive. If an extension of time with costs is agreed, the costs may be high if the prelims are high.
- Items that are likely to be omitted are priced low and items that are likely to increase are priced high.
- Items priced by unrealistically low provisional sums instead of a firm price could mean that that contractor will want a re-measure of the item based on actual cost during construction, and the price is bound to be higher than the provisional sum in the tender. Before accepting a tender with contractor provisional sums the contractor should be asked to measure and price the items in question as long as there is sufficient detail to measure.
- Multiple items costed as a lump sum and the word 'included' shown against numerous items can often be an indication that the tender has not been carefully priced. The danger is then that there will be no breakdown of cost against which to measure omissions and additions for these items during construction, or the contractor may try to argue that some specified items were not included in his tender. A poorly priced tender may also be an indication that there will also be sloppy work or poor practice on site.

Another thing to watch out for on the contractor's construction programme is if there is not enough work programmed in the early stages. The job is reported at site meetings as being on programme, but then towards the end, when too much work is programmed, the contractor will need more time and may try to justify an extension of time with costs. Even if additional costs are not agreed, this is annoying for the client, as it delays possession.

Traditional procurement and forms of contract

The construction contracts most widely used for traditional procurement on small projects are as follows:

- JCT Minor Works Building Contract
- JCT Minor Works Building Contract with Contractor Design
- JCT Building Contract for Homeowner/Occupier who has not appointed a consultant to oversee the work (HO/B)
- JCT Intermediate Contract
- JCT Intermediate Contract with Contractor Design
- RIBA Concise Building Contract (includes Contractor Design option)
- RIBA Domestic Building Contract (includes Contractor Design option)

ALWAYS CHECK YOU ARE USING THE CURRENT VERSION OF THE SELECTED CONTRACT AND MAKE SURE THE CONTRACT PRELIMINARIES REFER TO THE SAME VERSION OF THE CONTRACT.

If all the work your practice does is of a particular type and within certain financial limits you may be able to use the same contract on all your projects. This way you will become familiar with the content and better able to explain the contract to your clients – in particular the clauses relating to disputes, payment and insurance. When working with domestic clients it is important that you thoroughly explain the contract and have them confirm that they have understood it. Otherwise there is a risk that if something goes wrong a client might claim that the architect did not properly explain the relevant section in the contract.

FIGURE 10
Tender analysis for a small project where no QS is appointed.

ABC ARCHITECTS				
PROJECT ADDRESS:				
TENDER ANALYSIS				
REF: (JOB No) TENDER ANALYSIS				
Date:				
NBS CLAUSE	DESCRIPTION	PRE TENDER ESTIMATE	CONTRACTOR A	CONTRACTOR B	CONTRACTOR C
A10-A44	Preliminary Items (contractor to provide breakdown with tender)	10,800.00	13,500.00	incl in rates	5,500.00
	PROVISIONAL SUMS				
A54.114	Ground floor coat cupboard interior fittings	300.00	300.00	300.00	300.00
A54.115	Rebuild garden rear wall or replace with new fence	2,000.00	2,000.00	2,000.00	2,000.00
A54.116	Intruder alarm	600.00	600.00	600.00	600.00
A54.117	Replace kitchen floor screed or change heating to electric underfloor heating in kitchen	500.00	500.00	500.00	500.00
A54.113	Damp and timber treatment survey and works	1,100.00	1,100.00	1,100.00	1,100.00
A54.111	Supply of ironmongery	1,400.00	1,400.00	1,400.00	1,400.00
PRIME COST SUMS (CLIENT NOMINATED SUPPLIERS AND SUBCONTRACTORS)					
A54.110	Supply of sanitary fittings	3,905.00	3,905.00	3,905.00	3,905.00
A54.110	Profit %	390.00	585.75	390.00	390.50
A54.310	Supply and fit sliding doors	6,360.00	6,360.00	6,360.00	6,360.00
A54.310	Profit and attendance %	636.00	954.00	636.00	636.00
A54.311	Supply and fit new timber windows	11,250.00	11,250.00	11,250.00	11,250.00
A54.311	Profit and attendance %	112.50	1,687.50	1,125.00	1,125.00
A54.3120	Supply and fit new rooflights	6,805.00	6,805.00	6,805.00	6,805.00
	Profit and attendance %	680.50	1,020.75	680.50	680.50
A54.590	Contingency 6%	6,500.00	6,500.00	6,500.00	6,500.00
	Surveys (asbestos)	800.00	500 incl in C20	incl in C20	
C20	Demolition and strip out	4,000.00	7,183.00	3,400.00	4,650.00
D20	Excavation	2,500.00	3,101.00	2,400.00	3,850.00
E10,30,41	Concrete	2,500.00	2,577.00	2,400.00	3,250.00
F10,31	Brick, block and accessories	10,000.00	9,359.00	12,700.00	8,250.00
G12	Steel	2,000.00	292.00	1,900.00	1,000.00
G20	Carpentry, timber framing, first fixing	1,000.00	2,571.00	4,500.00	2,800.00
H71	Lead flashings	300.00	1,200.00	2,000.00	500.00
J30	Liquid damp proofing	300.00	738.00	800.00	500.00
J42	Sarna roof with 20-year guarantee	3,000.00	4,427.00	3,300.00	4,000.00
K10	Gypsum board wall and ceiling linings	6,000.00	3,778.00	5,400.00	3,250.00
K11	Ply roof deck, ply flooring	1,000.00	636.00	900.00	780.00
K21	Oak engineered floor, oak shelves, oak worktop to living units	6,000.00	7,667.00	6,500.00	5,410.00
	Living: Oak worktop to built in units, WC: oak shelves under basin, oak duct top	incl	incl	incl	1,000.00
L10	New timber windows (see PC Sum above)	0.00	0.00	0.00	0.00
L10	New rooflights (see PC Sum above)	0.00	0.00	0.00	0.00
L20	New hall door (see PC Sum above)	0.00	0.00	0.00	0.00
L20	Sliding doors (see PC Sum above)	0.00	0.00	0.00	0.00
L20	Internal doors	1,500.00	1,974.50	1,550.00	2,230.00
L30	Staircase works to balustrade incl oak capping	1,000.00	300.00	980.00	1,160.00
L40	Glazing (see PC Sum above)	200.00	600.00	0.00	0.00
M10	Screed	incl	810.00	1,800.00	2,870.00
M20	Plaster, render	1,500.00	1,660.00	4,600.00	2,870.00
M40	Floor and wall tiling	2,000.00	2,163.00	2,600.00	4,100.00
M60	Decoration	6,500.00	4,485.00	6,800.00	7,080.00
N10.11	Purpose made bathroom cabinet	2,000.00	2,200.00	2,000.00	1,300.00

Code	Description				
N10.12	Tiled removable bath panel	500.00	218.00	550.00	250.00
N10.13	Stone top to duct behind WC in bathroom	250.00	600.00	450.00	400.00
N10.14	TV and lighting recesses on living room wall	1,000.00	574.00	890.00	720.00
N10.16	Pull out laundry box	500.00	300.00	600.00	390.00
N10.86	Fireplace cladding to sides and front removable panel	500.00	479.00	760.00	350.00
N11.9	Fitted kitchen (incl appliances, worktops, splashbacks) CLIENT DIRECT ORDER	0.00	0.00		0.00
N11.9	Attendance by main contractor incl mechanical and electric	1,000.00	300.00	1,200.00	200.00
N13.9	Fix only sanitary fittings, accessories and heated towel rail (supply covered by PC Sum above)	1,200.00	810.00	1,600.00	1,460.00
P10	Insulation not priced elsewhere	300.00	430.00	900.00	580.00
P20	Skirtings, architraves, mirrors	800.00	1,257.00	800.00	1,120.00
P21	Fix only ironmongery incl in L10, L20 (supply covered by PC sum above)	500.00	incl	450.00	0.00
P30,31	Builders' work in connection with services	500.00	600.00	900.00	300.00
Q20,25	Stone paving and sub base	2,000.00	2,686.00	3,600.00	2,480.00
Q28	Topsoil	200.00	537.00	260.00	200.00
Q40	Rear garden: New 1.5m fence and gate to No6/No7 and No6/public footpath	2,000.00	3,100.00	2,000.00	2,750.00
R10	Rainwater drainage	300.00	130.00	600.00	410.00
R11	Foul drainage above ground	500.00	890.00	450.00	680.00
R12	Drainage below ground	1,000.00	1,350.00	900.00	1,000.00
S90	Hot and cold water supplies	3,000.00	3,725.00	2,500.00	1,000.00
S91	Gas	250.00	400.00	3,600.00	400.00
T90	Heating incl new boiler	7,000.00	9,328.00	4,600.00	5,320.00
U90	Mechanical extract and duct to kitchen and bathroom	800.00	660.00	650.00	680.00
V90	Electrical	7,500.00	10,039.00	6,500.00	7,350.00
V90	Supply of light fittings and bulbs	2,500.00	incl	2,800.00	2,200.00
W90	TV, smoke alarm	350.00	200.00	450.00	400.00
Z10-22	Workmanship clauses		incl	incl	incl
	CDM, H+S, etc	incl	incl	900.00	incl
	Contractor to price here for any items shown on drawings or in specification or deemed necessary but not included above	0.00	0.00	0.00	0.00
	Sub total	141,889.00	154,804.50	148,991.50	140,542.00
	VAT	28,377.80	30,960.90	29,798.30	28,108.40
	Total	170,266.80	185,765.40	178,789.80	168,650.40
CONTRACTOR TO PRICE HERE FOR RATES TO BE USED IN PRICING OF VARIATIONS AND /OR EXPENDITURE OF PROVISIONAL SUMS					
	Daywork rates for trades:				
	Plumber		300.00	250.00	200.00
	Electrician		300.00	250.00	200.00
	Carpenter		240.00	250.00	180.00
	Bricklayer		240.00	250.00	170.00
	Plasterer		240.00	250.00	170.00
	Tiler		200.00	250.00	170.00
	Decorator		180.00	250.00	140.00
	Labourer		150.00	200.00	120.00
	Variations: % mark up on materials		15%	10%	10%
	Start on site date confirmed as 7 Nov.		TBA	yes	yes
	Construction period: 17 weeks		TBA	yes	yes
	Confirmation of contract insurances provided		yes	yes	yes
	Breakdown of preliminaries provided		yes	yes	yes

FIGURE 11

Interim valuation

ABC ARCHITECTS
PROJECT:
VALUATION 1
REF: [Job No] Valuation 1
Date:

NBS CLAUSE	DESCRIPTION	ABC BUILDERS LTD.	VALUATION 1 (DATE.....) % COMPLETE	VALUATION 1 £
A10-A44	Preliminary Items (contractor to provide breakdown with tender)			
	Provisional Sums			
A54.115	Rebuild garden wall on rear boundary	2,000.00		0.00
A54.116	Intruder alarm	600.00		0.00
A54.117	Replace kitchen floor screed	500.00		0.00
A54.113	Damp and timber treatment	1,000.00		0.00
A54.111	Supply of ironmongery	1,400.00		
	Prime Cost Sums (Client nominated suppliers and sub contractors)			
A54.309	Supply of sanitary fittings	3,905.00		
A54.309	Profit %	390.50		
A54.310	Supply and fit sliding doors	6,360.00		
A54.310	Profit and attendance %	636.00		
A54.311	Supply and fit new timber windows	11,250.00		
A54.311	Profit and attendance %	112.50		
A54.312	Supply and fit rooflights	6,805.00		
A54.312	Profit and attendance %	680.50		
A54.590	Contingency	6,500.00		
	Surveys (asbestos)			incl
C20	Demolition and strip out	4,650.00	100	4,650.00
D20	Excavation	3,850.00	100	3,850.00
E10,30,41	Concrete	3,250.00	100	3,250.00
F10,31	Brick, block and accessories	8,250.00	40	3,300.00
G12	Steel	1,000.00	100	1,000.00
G20	Carpentry, timber framing, first fixing	2,800.00	0	0.00
H71	Lead flashings	500.00	0	0.00
J30	Liquid damp proofing	500.00	0	0.00
J42	Sarna roof with 20-year guarantee	4,000.00	0	0.00
K10	Gypsum board wall and ceiling linings	3,250.00	0	0.00
K11	Ply roof deck, ply flooring	780.00	0	0.00
K21	Oak engineered floor, oak shelves, oak worktop to living units	5,410.00	0	0.00
	Living: oak worktop to built in units, WC: oak shelves under basin, oak duct top	1,000.00	0	0.00
L10	New timber windows (see PC Sum above)	0.00	0	0.00
L10	New rooflights (see PC Sum above)	0.00	0	0.00
L20	New hall door (see PC Sum above)	0.00	0	0.00
L20	Sliding doors (see PC Sum above)	0.00	0	0.00
L20	Internal doors	2,230.00	0	0.00
	internal sliding door	incl	0	0.00
L30	Staircase works to balustrade incl oak capping	1,160.00	0	0.00
L40	Glazing (see PC Sum above)	0.00	0	0.00
M10	Screed	2,870.00	0	0.00
M20	Plaster, render	2,870.00	0	0.00
M40	Floor and wall tiling	4,100.00	0	0.00
M60	Decoration	7,080.00	0	0.00
N10.11	Purpose made bathroom cabinet	1,300.00	0	0.00
N10.12	Tiled removable bath panel	250.00	0	0.00
N10.13	Stone top to duct behind WC in bathroom		0	0.00
N10.14	TV and lighting recesses on living room wall	720.00	0	0.00
N10.16	Pull out laundry box	390.00	0	0.00
N10.86	Fireplace cladding to sides and front removable panel	350.00	0	0.00
N11.9	Fitted kitchen & dining & living units (incl appliances, worktops, splashbacks) - CLIENT DIRECT ORDER	0.00	0	0.00
N11.9	Attendance by main contractor incl mechanical and electric	200.00	0	0.00
N13.9	Fix only sanitary fittings, accessories and heated towel rail (supply covered by a PC Sum above)	1,460.00	0	0.00
P10	Insulation not priced elsewhere	580.00	0	0.00
P20	Skirtings, architraves, mirrors	1,120.00	0	0.00

Interim valuation

P21	Fix only ironmongery incl in L10, L20 (supply covered by PC Sum above)	0.00	0	0.00
P30,31	Builders' work in connection with services	300.00	0	0.00
Q20,25	Stone paving and sub base	2,480.00	0	0.00
Q28	Topsoil	200.00	0	0.00
Q40	Rear garden: New 1.5m fence and gate to No6/No7 and No6/public footpath	2,750.00	0	0.00
R10	Rainwater drainage	410.00	0	0.00
R11	Foul drainage above ground	680.00	0	0.00
R12	Drainage below ground	1,000.00	50	500.00
S90	Hot and cold water supplies	1,000.00	0	0.00
S91	Gas	400.00	0	0.00
T90	Heating incl new boiler	5,320.00	0	620.00
U90	Mechanical extract and duct to kitchen and bathroom	680.00	0	0.00
V90	Electrical	7,350.00	0	0.00
V90	Supply of light fittings and bulbs	2,200.00	0	0.00
W90	TV, smoke alarm	400.00	0	0.00
Z10-22	Workmanship clauses	incl	0	0.00
	CDM, H+S, etc			
	SITE INSTRUCTION 1			
	No cost items			
	SITE INSTRUCTION 2			
1	Omit PC Sum for sanitary fittings Add: Place order with Empress £3,905 + contractors 10% p+a (£4,295.50)		25% deposit paid	976.25
2	Omit: PC Sum for sliding doors Add: Place order with Fusion Glazing £6,360 + 10% p+a (£6,996.00)		50% deposit paid	3,180.00
3	Omit: PC Sum for timber windows Add: Place order with B Murphy £11,250 + 10% p+a (£12,375.00)		nothing paid	0.00
4	Omit: PC Sum for rooflights Add: Place order with Glazing Vision £6,805 + 10% p+a (£7,485.50)		50% deposit paid	3,118.75
	SITE INSTRUCTION 3			
1	No cost items			
	SITE INSTRUCTION 4			
1	Confirmation of Fusion drawing issue			
2	Add: Form 2 trial holes to expose footings		100	200.00
	SITE INSTRUCTION 5			
1	Confirmation of drawing issue - structure			
	Add: re-measure foundation			
	SITE INSTRUCTION 6			
1	Confirmation of drawing issue Add: remeasure drainage below ground as WD2 Rev 7 Materials: 1 x rodding point 1 x pipie 100mm x1.6 SP1 4 x flexseal standard coupling 110-121mm SC120 2 x 90o curved square section 1 x 450 oblique junction	453.16		150.00
1	Add: remeasure drainage below ground as WD2 Rev 7 Labour: remove brick manhole £360 extend existing clay drain to No7 £300 excavation work at No7 £120 new rodding installation at No7 £130 relay existing paving slabs at No7 £130 fix leaking elbow connection between clay pipe and svp metal pipe £150	1,190.00		300.00
	SITE INSTRUCTION 7			
1	Add: replace window hinges with fire escape hinges - 3 No windows	TBA		
	Omit: Bovingdon brick handmade rural multi (£1,000/1,000) x 3,000 bricks Add: Matchit stock brick G828/1 (£965/1,000) x 3,000 bricks	TBA		
2	Saving TBA			
	SUB TOTAL			**7,925.00**
	SUB TOTAL WITH 5% RETENTION			**7,528.75**
	LESS PREVIOUSLY PAID			**0**
	SUB TOTAL			**7,528.75**
	VAT @ 20%			**1,505.75**
	Total			**9,034.50**

Selecting a contractor and tendering using traditional procurement

RIBA STAGE		ITEM
0	STRATEGIC DEFINITION (project requirements)	Preliminary discussion with client on how contract can be procured.
1	PREPARATION AND BRIEF	Issue pre-contract programme showing key stages including tender and appointment of contractor. Obtain client agreement to procurement method recommended.
2	CONCEPT DESIGN	Update pre-contract programme.
3	DEVELOPED DESIGN	Update pre-contract programme.
4	TECHNICAL DESIGN	Complete the contract preliminaries, including reference to the selected contract. Select the contractors for the tender list. Confirm that the selected contractors are willing to tender. Issue tenders. Respond to queries from tendering contractors. Check and analyse tenders and make a recommendation to the client. If tenders are over-budget decide on action required. With client's agreement appoint a contractor and set a date for a pre-contract meeting. Client and contractor sign the contract that will be administered by the architect.
5	CONSTRUCTION	Administer the contract on behalf of the client.
6	HANDOVER AND CLOSE OUT (post-Practical Completion)	Administer the contract on behalf of the client.
7	STRATEGIC DEFINITION (project requirements in use)	N/A (the contract is completed at end of Stage 6)

Pre-contract meeting

The pre-contract meeting should be set up as soon as a contractor is appointed, and an agenda for the meeting should be issued to the contractor, the client and other consultants. If the type of work you do is repetitive you should have a standard agenda that can be quickly modified to include any particular items that are specific to the current project.

This meeting might be the first time your client and the contractor will sit around a table with you and discuss the project. The meeting should be minuted with action items that should be actioned before construction starts.

The pre-contract meeting should be held a minimum of two weeks prior to the start date to allow the contractor sufficient time to place orders, arrange labour, and issue the Construction Phase Plan, the construction programme and method statements. Time is also needed for both the contractor and the client to arrange the insurance cover required by the contract.

Client insurance

When domestic clients move out of a property during construction the arrangement of client insurance can be complicated. It is not always possible to extend existing building and contents insurance, and a new policy with a new insurance company may be the best option. This can take a few weeks for the client to sort out.

A word of warning: domestic clients can find the insurance clauses in contracts difficult to understand, and insurance can be difficult to obtain. Their insurance brokers will often confuse the matter further because they want to sell expensive new policies. Clients will often ask the architect to liaise with their insurance broker, but it is best to explain that the contract is clear about what insurance cover is required, that you as the architect are not an insurance expert, and clients should rely on the advice of their broker or the insurance company they deal with.

Ideally, all insurances should be in place before the pre-contract meeting. The contract should be signed and the signatures witnessed at the pre-contract meeting, and if this is not possible then at the latest the day before construction starts.

The agenda for the pre-contract meeting should be circulated in advance to give all parties time to prepare information and to add items to the agenda.

The agenda for a pre-contract meeting for the refurbishment of an existing dwelling might include the following items:

- Introductions
- Job contact sheet
- Contract (e.g. JCT Minor Works Building Contract)
- Contract period
- Date for possession
- Date for completion
- Contract sum
- Insurance details (contractor and client)
- Approvals
- Planning
- Listed building consent (if applicable)
- Freeholder approval (if applicable)
- Building Regulations plans approval
- Notice to building inspector of start on site date
- Party wall matters
- CDM: construction phase health and safety plan/method statement/ temporary works proposals
- Construction programme, including long orders, drawing submissions and subcontractor packages
- Cashflow forecast
- Occupancy by owner/Period of vacant possession
- Site foreman responsible for site supervision and quality control – name and mobile number
- Working hours
- Construction issue drawings (architect, structural engineer)
- Information required
- Variations and site instructions

- Site meetings/visits/inspections at key stages
- Valuations/Interim certificates/Payments/Cashflow forecast
- Condition surveys of adjoining properties/liaison with neighbours
- Skips and licence/Rubbish disposal/Keeping road and path clean/Hoardings
- Scaffolding and alarm
- Parking
- Asbestos survey
- Drains, sewers (existing)/CCTV survey
- Damp and timber infestation survey
- Record photos
- Client's belongings that will be on site
- Client direct orders
- Long-order items
- Client-supply items
- Named subcontractors
- Named suppliers
- Security
- Site security, alarms/keys
- Gas, water, electricity supplies
- Telephone, broadband, TV services
- Snagging
- Any other business

Site Instructions/Architect's Instructions

The contract will call for all instructions to be given by the architect and to be confirmed in writing and priced by the contractor within a time limit, usually seven days. The instructions given during the contract will be referred to as 'Site Instructions' or 'Architect's Instructions'. They will be priced by the contractor within seven days (or as stipulated in the contract), and the prices agreed with the architect or, on larger projects, with the quantity surveyor.

FIGURE 12
Site Instruction/
Architect's
Instruction

ABC ARCHITECTS
Address

Ref: (Job no.)..... SI 5
Date: ....

To: ABC Builders Limited
cc: File
        Client
        Structural engineer

Re: Address
SITE INSTRUCTION 5

1	**Structural Matters** Revised structural drawing showing existing surface water sewer and revisions to foundation design. Confirmation of drawing issue and calculations. Drawing ref: 7541/1A Calculations 10A, 11A, 12A, 13A (Drawing issue register, drawings and calculations attached to this instruction.) Works within 600mm of the sewers are **on hold** pending approval from Thames Water and issue of an updated build over licence.	£
2	**Trial Holes** Add: Dig two trial holes to expose the original footings under the flank wall and the party wall as shown on the sketch from the structural engineer 7541/SK100. (Drawing attached to this instruction.)	

Signed: (Architect)..

Date:..

The final account will be made up of the original tender items and the items listed on the architect's instructions.

In some cases, the architect may state on the instruction 'Cost to be agreed prior to construction'.

Instructions will only be issued in Stage 5 during construction, and a typical architect's instruction/site instruction can be set out as in the example opposite:

Site visits

Where work is carried out on an existing building and the construction is complex and the programme short, regular and frequent site visits during construction are important. On a small project such as a loft conversion, different trades move in and out of the building within days and defective existing or new construction can easily be covered, so site visits should be carried out weekly and, in addition, at key stages of construction.

As project/site architect, you should do the following:

- Note your site visit in the office diary, with the estimated time of your return to the office.
- Check the drawings before going to site and make notes of what should be checked on site.
- Have a mobile phone so you can be contacted when not in the office.
- Be suitably dressed to go on site, with site boots/shoes, hi-vis vest and, where appropriate, a hard hat.
- Be aware of and follow any site rules, such as signing in or wearing a hi-vis vest, and never go on site alone or out of working hours.
- Take to site a copy of the construction drawings and specification, and any instructions issued to date, and check the contractor has printed copies of all the latest-issue drawings on site.
- Take a camera, a measuring tape, a calculator and a spirit level to site as well as a pen and pad to take notes or make sketches.
- Note the date and who is present at the site meeting.

- Check the construction. If there is a lot to see it is sometimes best to ask the contractor to give you the time you need to look at the works before any discussion.

- Check that works are being carried out as shown on the drawings and as described in the specification and the Construction Phase Plan and method statements.

- Check progress against the construction programme.

- Check that the contractor has all the necessary information, and discuss what will happen during the coming week.

- Check that long-order items have been ordered in time to meet the programme.

- Check drawing submissions and approval dates for contractor design items.

- Take notes on site and on return to the office confirm any instructions in writing. Notes and sketches made on site should be kept in the job file.

- Ask the contractor (in the tender document) to take photographs of key stages of construction and to hand over the photos in digital format so they can be kept in the project archive. Check regularly with the contractor that the photos have been taken.

- Ask the building inspector to do a site visit at key stages of the construction to check excavations, reinforcement, drainage, damp-proof membrane/course continuity, steelwork erection, fire protection of steel, etc. The building inspector will issue site reports after every site visit, and these should be kept on file.

- Check that the contractor is not substituting specified products with products that are more readily available from their builder's merchant, for example insulation boards or damp-proof course.

It is easy to check good work on site that is well executed, and it is easy to condemn work that is badly executed or products that do not comply with the specification. It is, however, quite difficult to know what to do when work is almost acceptable yet not quite right. Any concerns should be noted and raised with the contractor straight away. If the issue cannot be resolved on site a decision should be made back at the office, perhaps with guidance from a colleague, on what further information or action is necessary – then instruct the contractor.

The RIBA's *Good Practice Guide: Inspecting Works* contains more detailed guidance for the site architect, suggesting how the eye can be trained to see as much as possible on site and what to look out for at every stage of construction.[20]

Site visits by the architect in traditional procurement

RIBA STAGE		ITEM
0	STRATEGIC DEFINITION (project requirements)	Verbal discussion with client on site.
1	PREPARATION AND BRIEF	Site visit to assess existing building. CAD dimensional survey of existing building carried out.
2	CONCEPT DESIGN	Hold client meetings on site and use the opportunity to collect more site information.
3	DEVELOPED DESIGN	Hold client meetings on site and use the opportunity to collect more site information.
4	TECHNICAL DESIGN	Further information collected on site if necessary. Visit site with tendering contractors. Arrange pre-contract meeting on site so contractors can see the site.
5	CONSTRUCTION	Carry out weekly site visits and additional visits as necessary.
6	HANDOVER AND CLOSE OUT (post-Practical Completion)	Attend site during the defects period if defects are urgent. Carry out inspection at the end of the defects liability period. Carry out final inspection on site to check that defects have been made good.
7	STRATEGIC DEFINITION (project requirements in use)	Stage 7 is post-contract. Client may ask the architect to carry out further inspections of the works post-contract, for example to investigate a suspected latent defect such as a roof leak.

When visiting sites pre-contract or during construction or post-contract, always follow the office health and safety policy procedure for site visits.

Extension of time/Liquidated and ascertained damages (LADs)

The contract will state the date for completion, and the main contractor's construction programme will show the same date for completion.

Extension of time

The client will sometimes delay the works by adding work to the contract during construction, or there might be a delay because a neighbour has not signed a party wall agreement, for example. When this happens the contractor should mitigate any delay but may become entitled to an extension of time, with costs in accordance with the construction contract. The costs must be based on actual losses, the works must be affected and delayed, and there must be no other contractual provision for reimbursement. The claim must be made at the proper time.

When the contractor claims for an extension of time full details should be provided, and the architect must assess the claim and grant the appropriate extension of time. The revised date for completion can be recorded on a site instruction, or you can issue a notification of revision to completion date. Costs will normally include the contractor's prelims for the extended period.

In order to properly assess a request for an extension of time it is important to have accurate records including site instructions, photographs of progress on site and a marked-up copy of the construction programme, showing when elements were actually started and completed.

Liquidated and ascertained damages (LADs)

If the contractor delays the works and does not meet the completion date, damages called liquidated and ascertained damages (LADs) can be levied from the contractor. However, these damages must be based on the client's actual losses arising out of the delayed completion, and the amount per week will be stated in the contract. For domestic work it may be difficult to assess the level of damages if the client is living in the property during construction. If the client is in rented accommodation, the rent and other actual costs would be included in the damages.

If the contractor fails to complete by the completion date, the architect must issue a non-completion certificate. If this certificate is not issued by the original completion date then it may not be possible to levy any damages from the contractor and the client could hold the architect responsible for any loss.

In reality, on many small domestic projects extensions of time are agreed with the client and the contractor at no extra cost to either party, because the client and the contractor may be jointly responsible for the delay and the contractor has covered the associated costs in his price for the variations. Any agreement relating to extensions of time must be confirmed in writing.

Certificates

A number of certificates will be issued during construction on site. The same format can be used for all the certificates, with the wording slightly altered for the different types of certificate. It is important to record the relevant dates on the certificates.

Certificates issued throughout the contract will include the following:

- STAGE 5 – Interim Certificate (issued with interim valuations and when the final account is agreed)
- STAGE 5 – Practical Completion Certificate (confirming date of Practical Completion)
- STAGE 5 – Non-Completion Certificate (if works are not completed within the contract period)
- STAGE 6 – Certificate of making good defects (confirming date defects have been made good)
- STAGE 6 – Final Certificate (certifying final release of retention)

On larger contracts, sometimes on domestic projects too, the works are handed over in phases and further certificates or statements are issued as follows:

- Statement of Retention (where more than one rate of retention applies)
- Section Completion Certificate (where part of the works are handed over)
- Statement of partial possession (where part of the works are handed over)
- Notification of revision to completion date

A typical interim certificate will look like the certificate shown in Figure 13.

FIGURE 13
Interim certificate

Issued by:	ABC Architects Ltd.
Address	....

Certificate for
INTERIM/PROGRESS PAYMENT

Employer:	....	Serial no:	(Job No)..... IC1
Address	....	Job reference:	(Job No)
Contractor:	ABC Builders Limited	Certificate no:	01
Address	....	Issue date:	
		Valuation date:	....

Works
Situated at: ....

Contract
dated: ....

Contract Sum: £...................................

This certificate for Interim/Progress payment is issued
under the terms of the above mentioned Contract

A.	Value of work executed and of materials and goods on site	£23,069.00
B.	Amount payable (95% of A)	£21,915.55
	Sub-total	£21,915.55
	Less amounts previously certified	-£0.00
	Net amount for payment	£21,915.55

We hereby certify that the amount for payment by the
Employer to the Contractor on this certificate is (in words)

Twenty one thousand nine hundred and fifteen pounds and
fifty five pence

Exclusive of VAT

Signed..
For ABC Architects

This is not a Tax Invoice
The contractor has given notice that the rate of VAT chargeable on the supply
of goods and services to which this certificate relates is 20% on £21,915.55.
Total of net amount and VAT amount is £26,298.66

Valuations, estimated final account and agreed final account

During the pre-contract stages (1–4) of a small project where no quantity surveyor is appointed, clients will rely on the budget advice provided by the architect. Once a contractor has been appointed (Stages 5–6) and a contract sum agreed, the client will rely on your valuations and your estimates of the final account to know what the likely total cost of the project will be. Some clients will take a fairly relaxed view as long as they are confident that the project is well managed and nothing significant has happened to increase the agreed contract sum. Other clients may want you to agree all costs in advance, have different options priced up and costed prior to instruction, request monthly final account estimates and then check and query items on every valuation.

On small jobs where the architect is providing all the cost information, it may be convenient to use the same spreadsheet for the pre-tender estimate, pricing tenders, valuations, final account estimates and final account. Your clients will become familiar with the format and find it much easier to follow the expenditure and any increase in cost during construction and when agreeing the final account.

Formats for pricing, valuations and final account will vary depending on the size and complexity of the project and whether or not a quantity surveyor is appointed, but whatever the size of the project the format used for valuations and final accounts should be fit for purpose, appropriate for the scale and value of the project and efficient to use, and if possible the same format should be used on all projects in the office.

FIGURE 14
Final account

	ABC ARCHITECTS	
	PROJECT: (Address)	
	FINAL ACCOUNT	
	REF: (Job No) FINAL ACCOUNT	
	Date:	

NBS CLAUSE	DESCRIPTION	ABC BUILDERS LTD
A10-A44	Preliminary Items	4,900.00
A54	PROVISIONAL SUMS	
A54.110	Additional structural work	omitted
A54.110a	Supply of ironmongery	omitted
A54.111	Additional repairs to timber structure	omitted
A54.112	Additional plastering	omitted
A54.113	Replacement of incoming water main	omitted
A54.521	DPC Injection by specialist	omitted
A54.590	Contingency	omitted
C20	Asbestos survey	150.00
C20	CCTV Drainage survey - 250.00	omitted
C20	Strip out and demolition	5,780.00
C45	DPC chemical injection (see prov sums above)	0.00
C90.10	Alterations to exisitng staircase	1,680.00
C90.11	External seal to existing windows	370.00
C90.12	Fireplace and hearth in living	650.00
D20	Excavation	3,500.00
E10,30,41	Concrete and reinforcement	2,800.00
F10,30,31	Brick walling, accessories, sills lintels, re-pointing, flaunching, isolated repairs to brick walls	7,900.00
G12	Steel structure	2,300.00
G20	First fix carpentry	700.00
H65	Roof tiling (new vents)	350.00
H71	Lead sheet and flashings	700.00
J30	Liquid damp proofing	incl
J42	Roofing (Sarna)	3,500.00
K10	Plasterboard, dry linings (ceilings, stud walls, thermal board, vertical boarding)	8,500.00
K11	Ply flooring and roof decking	1,500.00
K21	New oak flooring to ground floor	3,250.00
L10	Rooflight	3,300.00
L20	Velfac doors and window	3,200.00
L20	Internal doors	1,700.00
L30	Loft access and ladder (see below)	0.00
M10	Screed	priced below
M20	Specialist render, make good wall plaster and skim, replace 25m² wall plaster	2,200.00
M40	Tiling to bathroom walls and kitchen splashback	1,680.00
M50	Sheet flooring and carpet	1,800.00
M60	Decoration	5,900.00
N11.	Assemble and fix only Ikea kitchen and appliances supplied by client	650.00
N13	Supply and fit sanitary fittings incl wastes, traps	3,450.00
P10	Insulation (not measured elsewhere) including ground floor between joists	900.00
P20	Skirting architrave and trims, sundry items incl elecricty cupboard	2,900.00
P21	Ironmongery (supply covered by a PC Sum, fitting included in L10, L20)	0.00
P31	Builders' work in connection with services	600.00
Q40	Fencing	350.00
R10	Rainwater drainage system	650.00
R11	Above ground foul drainage	760.00
R12	Below ground drainage (incl Aco linear drain, new manhole cover)	1,460.00
S90	Hot and cold water supplies	2,300.00
S91	Gas supplies	230.00
T90	Heating incl new boiler and radiators	3,200.00
U90	Ventilation	priced below
V90	Electrical (incl supply of light fittings and bulbs)	4,500.00
W90	TV, smoke alarm	500.00
Z10,12,,20,21	Workmanship clauses	incl
	The contractor to price here for any work shown or described but not included above	0.00
M10	Screed	incl
L30	Loft ladder and access hatch	350.00
U90	Bathroom extract, kitchen extract duct, roof terminals	incl
C45.3	Chemical injection by Proten and associated Builders' work (404.00)	see SI 8.1
	Sub total	**91,110.00**
	SITE INSTRUCTION 1	
4	Add: 1 no telephone point	75.00

	SITE INSTRUCTION 2		
2	Omit: Sarna roofing Add: Fatra roofing		-300.00
3	Add: replace flat roof to return including joists		2,700.00
5	Omit: Glazing Vision roogflight Add: Roofglaze rooflight		-1,000.00
	SITE INSTRUCTION 3		
1	Add: revised foundation design		1,350.00
2	Add: new radiator and pipework to bedroom 1, 2 new radiators and pipework etc to bedroom 2		1,140.00
	SITE INSTRUCTION 4		
2	Add: 1 No dsso		75.00
4	Add: remove live wall plaster on masonry walls (over the 25m^2 included at tender stage)		200.00
	Add: 29m^2 new plasterboard on studs with insulation between		750.00
	Add: 16m^2 renew plaster / render to masonry walls (over the 25m^2 included at tender stage)		800.00
	Add: 41m^2 board over live lath and plaster on stud walls		650.00
	Add: Board over plasterboard where paper cannot be removed	incl above	
	Add: Thermal lining to bedroom 1 window wall		1,200.00
	Add: Thermal lining to bedroom 2 window wall		800.00
	Omit: 86m^2 making good to plaster and new skim coat incl in tender and incl in new work above. Omit waterproof render and skim coat to front bedroom wall		-1,600.00
	SITE INSTRUCTION 5		
1	Add: support to purlins		50.00
2	Add: Form trial hole 2 as requested by Thames Water		200.00
	SITE INSTRUCTION 6		
1	Confirmation brick up to ground level can be semi engineering brick		-100.00
2	Retain original picture rails to living and dining / replace if replastering		0.00
3	Add: Carefully remove and set aside original cupboards in dining	100.00	
	SITE INSTRUCTION 7		
1	Add: Supply and fit new beam under the bathroom chimney breast and concrete pads		200.00
	SITE INSTRUCTION 8		
1	Add: Place order with Proten - Spray all accessible timbers incl ground floor void and roof etc.		2,979.30
1	Contractors 10% on Proten order		297.93
	SITE INSTRUCTION 9		
2	Add: Builders' work in connection with Proten - replace timbers with wet rot		620.00
2	Add: Fit new concrete lintel over bathroom window to fill void		90.00
4	Add: Extend fireplace opening vertically to form shelf recess		400.00
	SITE INSTRUCTION 10		
1	Add: ground floor: replace rotten plates and 1 No short joist	120.00	
	SITE INSTRUCTION 11		
	SITE INSTRUCTION 12 REV 1		
4	Add: Ground floor: retrofit DPC on sleeper walls under existing plates		60.00
5	Add: re-screed hearths to living and dining		50.00
6	Obtain and Complete forms from Affinity Water then obtain quote for new water supply from Affinity (£241.78 + 10%) Affinity (£241.78 paid by client)		24.17
	SITE INSTRUCTION 13		
2	Confirmation of tile spec		-50.00
4	Add: supply washing machine (£499 + 10%)		549.00
8	Clarification - shower ref		300.00
	SITE INSTRUCTION 14		
2	Add: Tricoya mdf board in bathroom - omit MR mdf		200.00
5	Add: 4 paint samples		24.00
	SITE INSTRUCTION 15		
4	Add: replace moulding to hall door bottom 2 panels		100.00
	SITE INSTRUCTION 16		
6	Ironmongery re measure cost (185.76) + 10% (based on invoices)		204.33
12	Add: shaver point		100.00
13	Add: Study replace glass with new double glazed unit		100.00
16	Add: Bedroom 1 window repair masonry cill		50.00
	SITE INSTRUCTION 17		
2	Add: Asbestos removal by Ace + 10% (300 + 30)		330.00
3	Add: supply and fit porch light, bulb		95.00
6	Add: Place order with Affinity Water for a new supply Add: Contractors 10% Add: Builders' work in connection with new supply		1,791.78
	Contractors 10% on Affinity quote		179.78
	Excavation and new pipe, duct, holes etc		300.00
	Disconnect old supply and cap off, remove temporary pipework and connect new pipe incl stopcocks etc.		300.00
		Sub total	**107,615.29**
		VAT @ 20%	**21,523.06**
		Total	**129,138.35**

Health and Safety File/Building Manual

The purpose of the Health and Safety File/Building Manual is to provide the client at Practical Completion with the relevant certificates, guarantees, instructions and information necessary to safely run and maintain the property. It is also a record of what works have been undertaken and by whom. The file is held on the premises and should be updated during any further works on the property. On a domestic project the file will contain more information than the minimum health and safety information required under the CDM Regulations (see page 140).

At Practical Completion, the principal designer (usually the architect) will compile and hand over the Health and Safety File/Building Manual to the client. The principal contractor will provide most of the information required. Designers will provide the relevant latest construction issue or as-built drawings. The information provided by the principal contractor should be handed to the principal designer a minimum of one week prior to Practical Completion so the documents can be checked and the complete updated document handed to the client at Practical Completion.

IF A PRINCIPAL DESIGNER HAS NOT BEEN APPOINTED THROUGH TO PRACTICAL COMPLETION, THE PRINCIPAL CONTRACTOR IS REQUIRED UNDER THE CDM REGULATIONS TO COMPILE AND HAND OVER THE HEALTH AND SAFETY FILE TO THE CLIENT.

Health and Safety File/Building Mannual – contents for a domestic project

- contents page
- description of the building
- description of the works
- names and contact details
  - principal designer and principal contractor – CDM
  - consultants (designers)
  - main contractor and subcontractors (note design responsibility if applicable)
  - contractors working directly for the client (note design responsibility if applicable)
- start and completion date
- date of practical completion
- building regulations completion certificate
- electrical certificate
- gas safety certificate
- boiler installation certificate
- asbestos survey (and invoice for asbestos removal if applicable)
- guarantees/warranties/leaflets/maintenance instructions
- as-built drawings or latest construction issue drawings
  - architect's drawings and schedules
  - specialist subcontractor/contractor design drawings.

As-built drawings

At the end of Stage 5 – Practical Completion – the architect will hand over to the client the Health and Safety File/Building Manual and a set of drawings. Although the term 'as-built' is widely used it is more correct to issue these drawings as 'latest construction issue' because, strictly speaking, only the contractor knows exactly what has been built. It is only necessary to provide drawings that may be of use to the client and the number of drawings will depend on the scope of the works. For a domestic project these drawings might include the following:

- structural drawings
- site plan showing drainage and boundaries
- floor plans showing sanitary fittings, plant and services (stopcocks, gas, heating, hot water, power, lighting and drainage)
- roof plan
- sections
- elevations
- schedule of finishes
- schedule of electrical fittings
- schedule of sanitary fittings
- schedule of radiators
- schedule of appliances
- schedule of doors, windows and ironmongery.

Some of the above drawings may be contractor design drawings or specialist subcontractors' drawings.

As an architect carrying out small projects you are likely to receive many phone calls from previous clients wanting to know what colour paint was used for a particular space, or what type of light bulb they should buy to replace the bulb in a light fitting, or the reference for a heated towel rail so the valve can be replaced, for example. You can refer the client to the Health and Safety File/Building Manual, where all this information should be available. Alternatively, you should be able to quickly check this information for your client from the digital file for the particular project, even if it was completed some years ago.

An efficient and helpful response to such requests from previous clients will not only help your clients but it may also be the service that puts your practice in mind when your clients hear that a family member or a friend is looking for a good architect.

Snagging and defects

Snagging

Small contractors on domestic projects will often invite the architect to snag the works before they are complete, expecting the architect to be a finishing foreman who will make a list of incomplete items and also give the contractor an early indication of the standard expected. It is a good idea to put snagging on the pre-contract meeting agenda, and make it clear to the contractor before the works commence that the works must be complete and cleaned before snagging can commence. A period for snagging and clearing snagging items should also be included on the contract programme.

Small contractors on domestic projects will also ask for Practical Completion when there are items remaining on the snagging list, especially if the client has moved back into the property or did not move out. Unless there is a good reason why not, all items on the snag list should be cleared before Practical Completion is granted.

Inspect the works then issue one snag list to the contractor, incorporating any items the client has picked up and including any paperwork that is required.

When the contractor has cleared all the items on the snag list carry out an inspection to check the works are complete and invite the client to check with you and agree that a Practical Completion certificate can be issued. Remind your client that from the date of Practical Completion the client's insurance will take over from the contractor's insurance.

Handover

Before arranging the handover meeting with the client check all of the following:

- That the works are complete.
- That all snagging items have been cleared.
- That builders' plant and materials have been removed from site.
- That the Building Regulations completion certificate has been issued.
- That services have been commissioned.
- That a thorough clean is complete.
- That the Health and Safety File/Building Manual is complete.

At the handover meeting with the contractor and the client:

- Inspect the works with the client (if not already inspected) and confirm that the works are complete.
- If there are any elements of work that are not complete, discuss with the client whether they can be completed after Practical Completion.
- Confirm the date of Practical Completion.
- Ensure that the contractor returns all sets of keys to the client.
- Demonstrate to the client how all the mechanical or electrical equipment, including heating controls, alarms, etc., works.
- Explain responsibilities during the defects liability period.
- Remind the client that their insurance must be in place from the date of Practical Completion.
- Hand over the Health and Safety File/Building Manual, including leaflets, maintenance instructions, guarantees and warranties. Explain the document to the client and also their responsibility under the CDM Regulations to make the file available should they carry out further works on the property.
- Explain to the client that the contractor will attend to any urgent defects (such as leaks or failure of equipment) during the defects period, but that non-urgent defects should be sorted out at the end of the defects period.

Defects

Most construction contracts will have a defects liability period after Practical Completion, which will normally be six or twelve months. During the defects liability period urgent items should be dealt with immediately by the contractor, such as leaks, or equipment or fittings that are noisy or do not work. All other items, such as shrinkage cracks, should be left until the end of the defects liability period.

At the end of the defects liability period the architect should arrange with the client to carry out an inspection and issue a list of defects. Clients should be asked to keep a list of any defects they notice during the liability period. This could be a light that flickers or a kitchen plinth that falls down or a floorboard that squeaks, for example – things that might not be noted by an architect when carrying out a site inspection. The list can be given to the architect before the inspection, and the items included on the list. It is best for the architect to compile one list including any items the client has picked up, rather than the architect issuing one list and the client a separate list. The client should always liaise with the contractor through the architect.

As soon as the items on the defects list have been cleared, a final inspection should be made. A final certificate is then issued, releasing the final balance of the retention – normally 2.5%.

Project archive

You should not archive projects until Stage 6, after the issue of the certificate releasing the final retention. When the project is ready to archive the files should be thinned down to the information that will be retained for a minimum of six years, but preferably twelve years or even longer.

The documents can be in paper or digital form. Copies of all correspondence by email during the contract should also be retained. In the event of a claim, email correspondence can be vital to establish relevant dates. The archive should also include copies of all photographs taken during construction, as these could be vital in the event of a claim or to investigate a latent defect. The information in the project archive will depend on the scope of the project, but on a domestic project will almost always include some or all of the following.

Project archive list

- job number
- address
- contact list
- signed architect's appointment
- approvals
- planning application and permission
- listed building consent
- building regulations plans approval
- build over agreement from Thames Water (if applicable)
- freeholder approval (if applicable)
- key correspondence with the client
- original signed JCT or RIBA construction contract (or copy)
- site notes
- building regulations completion certificate
- electrical certificate
- boiler installation certificate
- gas safety certificate
- guarantees
- DPC, damp and timber treatment
- windows/doors and glazing
- roof
- surveys
- asbestos
- drains
- contractor's tender
- tender analysis
- contractor's insurance
- client's insurance
- final account
- site instructions
- tender document
- record drawings and schedules
- party wall agreements
- progress photos
- emails.

IDEALLY THE PROJECT ARCHIVE SHOULD BE STORED IN A SEPARATE LOCATION TO THE OFFICE. IN THE EVENT OF A FIRE OR FLOOD, THE ARCHIVES WOULD NOT BE DAMAGED OR LOST.

It is acceptable to keep some or all of the above information on a digital device, as long as there is a further backup copy elsewhere.

Archives can be stored in various ways, all of which are acceptable. What is important is to have all the relevant information and to be able to retrieve information efficiently.

A summary sheet listing the project archives should be kept up to date with a copy in the office manual, so the location of any project archive can be accessed with ease by anyone in the office.

What makes a project successful?

Subject to appointment, the architect is responsible for taking the project through Stages 0–7 and checking at each stage that the client is satisfied with the design, the budget, the programme and the services provided by all members of the team, including the contractor.

Success could mean any or all of the following achievements:

- Everyone enjoyed working on the project.
- Your client is delighted with the end result.
- The design has worked well and the photos will look good on your website.
- The project is published or wins an award.
- The quality of the construction is excellent.
- The project was completed within budget.
- The project was completed on time.
- The architect and the contractor made a reasonable profit on the job.
- New skills were acquired.
- Good consultants or contractors were found who will work with the practice again.
- The client has recommended you to potential new clients.

Feedback

Do not wait until the project is finished and handed over to get feedback from your client. It is better to get feedback at the end of each stage, so if your client has any concerns they can be addressed and the same concern will not arise during the next stage. Things do go wrong and difficulties do arise on projects, especially small domestic projects. It is how you handle these situations that matters.

Teamwork

Be positive with your clients and remember that what is a small domestic project for your practice may be a huge project for your clients. See things from their point of view and help them to enjoy the process of design and construction.

Be mindful of your responsibility as the architect to pull the project and the team together, and be generous in your recognition of the contribution of all the members of the team on each project – including the client, the consultants, the contractor and subcontractors – because they all have a vital role to play in the success of 'your' project!

> **Part 4**
Case Studies

Arnold House Primary School

LOCATION: NW8, London

PROJECT: Extension at roof level

CLIENT: Arnold House School

ARCHITECT: Marianne Davys Architects

STRUCTURAL ENGINEER: Heyne Tillett Steel

QUANTITY SURVEYOR: Batey Associates

CONTRACTOR: Newland Construction

SPECIALIST GLASS CONTRACTOR: Cantifix

CONSTRUCTION COST: £387,000 + VAT

CONTRACT: JCT Minor Works Building
Contract with Contractor Design

DATE COMPLETED: 2013

▶ Project Brief

The existing building is a primary school on
a residential street in a conservation area of
Westminster. The school is composed of two
original houses, a link building and an extension to
the rear with limited external play area.

The brief was to provide two new classrooms and
two new practice rooms, and to identify where
on the school premises the new accommodation
could be located.

▶ Project specifics

The original idea to build at roof level was
developed with the school bursar, and then
a feasibility study – including preliminary
discussions with Westminster Council – was
presented to the Board of Governors before the
full project was commissioned.

The original roof was completely removed and the ceiling heights of the existing first-floor classrooms were reduced to gain headroom above. A new steel frame was built, with a flat roof and sloping pitches clad in the original roof tiles, so the appearance of the building on the front elevation was unaltered. The new classrooms are lit by dormers on the rear elevation, conservation roof lights on the side elevations and large roof lights on the flat roof, where solar panels that provide water heating are also located.

To obtain planning permission, it was necessary to convince planning that the corridor link to the rest of the school at eaves level was subservient to the original building. For this reason, frameless glazing was used and the new construction is well set back from the front elevation.

▶ Project challenges

- There was a need to identify where on the school premises the new accommodation could be located.

- There was a need to obtain planning consent from Westminster to build at roof level in a conservation area with strict guidelines controlling what was considered acceptable.

- There was a need to build above the existing school within a short construction period with a fixed completion date, and for part of the project to be undertaken during term time.

- The frameless glass extension required a road closure and a crane to lift the glazing, as well as a very accurate survey and drawings, and a skilled specialist team on site.

Holland Park Avenue

LOCATION: W11, London

PROJECT: Refurbishment with basement

CLIENT: Private domestic client

ARCHITECT: Marianne Davys Architects

STRUCTURAL ENGINEER: Charles Harris & Partners

QUANTITY SURVEYOR: Batey Associates

PARTY WALL SURVEYOR: James Davidson

CONTRACTOR: Cubitt Theobald

JOINERY: Cubitt Theobald

CONSTRUCTION COST: £725,000 + VAT

CONTRACT: JCT Intermediate Building Contract with Contractor Design

DATE COMPLETED: 2015

▶ Project brief

The existing Regency-style house was built in the 1820s in the Ladbroke Conservation Area of the Royal Borough of Kensington and Chelsea. The house has three storeys, plus a basement.

The brief was to refurbish the house and gardens, retain as many of the original features as possible and provide a comfortable and light-filled family home, with open-plan reception rooms on the ground floor and open-plan kitchen and dining at basement level, opening on to a garden terrace.

▶ Project specifics

The house was in a very poor state of repair, both internally and externally. The house had been altered internally in the 1950s and later extended to the rear with a single-storey flat-roof extension. The gardens were overgrown and the original basement was dark and damp with low ceilings.

The extension to the rear was demolished, restoring the house to its original footprint and the garden to its original size. Extensive masonry repair and temporary structural works were required before the internal structural alterations and basement excavation could commence. Some of the original features had been lost, such as the entrance porch, and this was replaced. However, some original features had survived, and these were all carefully restored as part of the project. Window sashes were replaced to carefully match the original proportions, but with double glazing and acoustic glass to provide insulation from the road noise. Large glass doors were installed at basement level, and on the upper floors some small sash windows on the rear elevation were replaced with French doors, internal shutters and external balustrades.

The success of the project depended to a large extent on the quality and attention to detail in both design and manufacture of the purpose-made joinery and metalwork. To this end, many of the contractor design drawings – for example the internal shutters – were printed and checked at 1:1 scale.

▶ Project challenges

- The extent of temporary and permanent structural work required.
- The need to provide a garden terrace below the level of the existing drains.
- The party wall agreements with adjoining owners.
- Finding the right contractor for the project with an in-house joinery works.

Mansfield Street

LOCATION: W1, London

PROJECT: Refurbishment

CLIENT: Private domestic client

ARCHITECT: Marianne Davys Architects

M+E ENGINEER: David Miles & Partners

CONTRACTOR: Creese & McKnight

CONSTRUCTION COST: £270,000 + VAT

CONTRACT: JCT Minor Works Building Contract

DATE COMPLETED: 2015

▶ Project brief

The exceptionally large south- and west-facing London apartment is on the third floor of a Grade II-listed 1930s mansion block close to Oxford Circus.

The brief was to replace the windows and refurbish the interior with energy-efficient and low-maintenance lighting, new kitchen and bathrooms, new fireplace, and built-in bookshelves and wardrobes, whilst preserving many original features, as well as features from a previous refurbishment.

▶ Project specifics

The property was in relatively good condition, but the single-glazed inward-opening windows leaked, and noise from the street was a problem. The interior needed internal alterations to make it easy to maintain for an elderly couple, and to accommodate the client's collection of paintings and books.

The project required a good understanding of the original building, the apartment and the communal areas, and a sensitive approach to design.

Westminster Council also wished to keep as many original features as possible, so when it came to the windows permission was given to replace the inward-opening casements, but the frames had to be refurbished in situ using original ironmongery. It would have been easier and more cost-effective to fit new windows manufactured off site. Due to the freeholder's restriction on external scaffolding, a special internal scaffold was designed so the window frames could be safely refurbished and painted inside and out from the inside. A request was made for planning permission to use acoustic glass in the new double-glazing, which was granted by the conservation officer as long as no visual differences were discernable. As the property is on the third floor and no difference could be seen at street level, permission was granted and acoustic glass was fitted in all windows, significantly reducing noise from the street.

▶ Project challenges

- Obtaining planning permission and listed building consent from Westminster Council to replace the windows with double-glazed acoustic glass.

- Keeping the original 1930s light fittings, but replacing and colour matching the original light source of the fittings with new LED lighting.

- Working on site with occupied properties above, below and either side of the apartment.

- Working within the freeholder's restrictions and rules for contractors that did not allow the erection of external scaffolding or use of the main lift. There was nowhere on site for rubbish pending collection, and the communal areas had to be kept clear and clean at all times.

- Finding a contractor who would comply with all the restrictions above and stay on good terms throughout the project with the porters in the building and many adjoining owners.

Springfield Avenue

LOCATION: N10, London

PROJECT: Refurbishment with ground floor and basement extension

CLIENT: Marianne Davys

ARCHITECT: Marianne Davys Architects

STRUCTURAL ENGINEER: Charles Harris & Partners

PARTY WALL SURVEYOR: James Davidson

CONTRACTOR: Domi Development

CONSTRUCTION COST: £200,000 + VAT

CONTRACT: JCT Minor Works Building Contract

DATE COMPLETED: 2015

▷ Project brief

The property is a 1950s semi-detached ex-council house with gardens to the front and rear. The house is at the end of a cul-de-sac on a south-facing sloping site, next to Alexandra Palace and with panoramic views of London.

The brief was to provide a self-contained studio basement extension at ground-floor level, to alter and extend the ground floor of the property using the roof of the basement extension as a terrace outside the new kitchen and dining areas, and to provide a roof terrace at first-floor level accessed from the master bedroom.

▷ Project specifics

A public sewer running behind the house had to be avoided, so the new basement is two metres away from the footprint of the original house.

Although the slope reduced the amount of excavation needed to the basement, this was still

a significant exercise. An excavator at garden level did most of the digging, and two separate conveyor belts carried the dense clay to a compound at street level, from where it was removed daily over a period of five weeks. The excavator then exited the garden via a purpose-made ramp to the council-owned allotments to the rear of the property.

By establishing the existing water table level and using the natural slope of the land, there was no need for pumped surface water drainage. Surface water in the rear garden is taken to a soakaway under the lawn.

Apart from maximising enjoyment of the sun and the views, the benefit of the roof terrace at first floor level is its function as an alternative means of escape that enables a more open-plan arrangement on the ground floor.

The ground-floor extension with a sedum roof is highly insulated, and the original ground-floor structure was replaced with new insulation and underfloor heating, so although the house has increased in area by one-third the heating bills have increased by a relatively smaller amount.

Good relations with neighbours were crucial and all were patient and understanding about the temporary loss of parking, the noise and dust, and the daily deliveries of materials. An almost identical project was carried out for the adjoining owners.

▶ Project challenges

- Obtaining planning permission for roof terraces.
- Access for the excavator and removal of the waste material to street level with a series of conveyor belts.
- To meet the fire regulations, given the open-plan internal layout.
- To provide the new basement accommodation at garden level without the need for pumps.
- To design around a public sewer that ran behind the original house.
- The architect was living and working in the house during construction and the loft-level office looks straight down on the site – a challenge for the contractor!

Hillfield Park

LOCATION: N10, London

PROJECT: Full refurbishment with extension at ground floor and basement

CLIENT: Private domestic client

ARCHITECT: Marianne Davys Architects

STRUCTURAL ENGINEER: Charles Harris & Partners

QUANTITY SURVEYOR: Batey Associates

PARTY WALL SURVEYOR: James Davidson

CONTRACTOR: Talina Builders

CONSTRUCTION COST: £620,000 + VAT

CONTRACT: JCT Intermediate Building Contract with Contractor Design

DATE COMPLETED: 2015

▶ Project brief

The three-storey Edwardian terraced house is in a conservation area in the London Borough of Haringey, on a steep hill with a tiny front garden and a long rear garden. The rear faces south, and at roof level there are panoramic views.

The brief was to refurbish and extend the property into a comfortable family home, to create a recording studio in an enlarged basement, and also a bright open-plan kitchen/dining/living space opening on to a garden with a water feature and raised planters.

▶ Project specifics

The house was in a very poor state of repair internally and externally. The ground floor in particular was dark with small rooms and corridors, and the basement was damp with

insufficient headroom. Extensive temporary works were required before the structural alterations, excavation and refurbishment could commence.

On the ground floor, the house was extended into the garden to the site boundaries. The loft was converted and extended with a dormer. The basement was excavated, tanked, insulated and soundproofed. Internally, load-bearing and non-load bearing walls were removed to provide a bright open-plan kitchen. To maximise light, the extension was built in frameless triple-glazing with large sliding/folding doors opening on to the garden. In the side extension, opening rooflights provided further light and natural ventilation close to the cooking area.

The first-floor balcony is also accessed by fully glazed folding doors that can be left open during fine weather, so the terrace and garden become part of the space.

▶ Project challenges

- To obtain planning permission for the extension and alterations. Permission was refused for the proposed roof terrace and it was omitted from the project.

- Temporary works and extensive structural alterations were required to achieve the open-plan space at basement and ground-floor level.

- Numerous party wall agreements were required as the adjoining properties were multi-occupancy.

- Excavation and underpinning for the basement, as the house was on a steep hill and in poor condition.

- Soundproofing was needed in the basement to prevent outside noise affecting recording, and music from bothering neighbours.

- Meeting fire regulations was a challenge; a mist fire protection system was installed.

- The design and construction of a sustainable water feature; the water is recycled.

Clink Street

LOCATION: E1, London

PROJECT: Internal fit-out

CLIENT: Private domestic client

ARCHITECT: Marianne Davys Architects

QUANTITY SURVEYOR: Batey Associates

STRUCTURAL ENGINEER: Whitby & Bird

VAT CONSULTANT: Landmark PT

CONTRACTOR: Miles Building

CONSTRUCTION COST: £295,000 + VAT

CONTRACT: JCT Agreement for Minor Building Works

DATE COMPLETED: 2004

▶ Project brief

The existing apartment is on the top floor and includes the double pitched roof space of a Grade II-listed 19th-century warehouse building, with elevations on Clink Street and the River Thames, close to Southwark Cathedral.

The brief was to fit out the interior to provide three bedrooms and bathrooms, a library, a utility room, ancillary spaces and storage at a new mezzanine level on the street side, and a large open-plan full-height office/living/dining/kitchen space on the river side. The brief also included opening conservation roof lights above the exposed roof trusses to increase the amount of light throughout the apartment, and fitting secondary windows with acoustic glass on the street side.

▶ Project specifics

On the north-facing river side, the space is open plan for the full length of the apartment, using furniture and built-in units to define the areas for office, living, dining and kitchen. The central part of the plan contains stairs, lift, library, utility room, bathroom and WC. The individual bedrooms and an ensuite bathroom are located on the noisy south-facing street side, and in these rooms secondary windows with acoustic glass were fitted. Mezzanine spaces were created in the roof space above the bedrooms as study and storage areas.

The large opening roof lights above the original rafters on the south side of the pitched roof over the kitchen/dining/living/office area transform the space, allowing sunlight and ventilation to the space below.

Internal timber wall-cladding and timber boarded doors are detailed in a traditional way and painted in a wide palette of colours selected by the client,

while standalone elements such as the stainless-steel kitchen island and the extractor above are modern and minimalist. The client's collection of artwork, paintings and antique furniture seem just right for this unique space.

▶ Project challenges

- Prolonged discussions with Southwark Council throughout the project to obtain approval for the new roof lights, the secondary windows and the alterations to the original structure.

- Meeting the client's brief while minimising any alteration to the original structure.

- The location on Clink Street made it difficult and time-consuming for the contractor to move all the rubbish out of the building, to have the rubbish collected or materials delivered, and to carry materials up the stairs to the top floor.

Buckley Road

LOCATION: NW6, London

PROJECT: Refurbishment and extension

CLIENT: Private domestic client

ARCHITECT: Marianne Davys Architects

STRUCTURAL ENGINEER: Charles Harris & Partners

PARTY WALL SURVEYOR: James Davidson

CONTRACTOR: Aran Construction

CONTRACT: JCT Minor Works Building Contract

CONSTRUCTION COST: £116,000 + VAT

DATE COMPLETED: 2013

▶ Project brief

The existing one-bedroom flat with rear garden and basement utility room is on the ground floor of a three-storey Victorian terraced house that has been converted into four flats.

The brief for the project was to refurbish the property to provide an extra bedroom, and to build a large ground-floor extension to provide open-plan kitchen/dining/living.

▶ Project specifics

What the client wanted to build was relatively straightforward and was a good way of increasing the value of the property, but the budget was tight and the proposed extension to the leasehold property required numerous approvals – there was a strong chance that one or more of the

approvals would not be granted. The client was lucky that freeholder approval was granted, that none of the leaseholders or adjoining owners objected, and that planning approval was granted and party wall agreements were all signed after successful negotiations with the adjoining owners.

The front living room was converted into a bedroom, the rear bedroom was retained, the bathroom required no work, the original basement was tanked and refurbished as a utility room, and the large extension provided an open plan kitchen/dining/living area with a wood-burning stove. The original kitchen was left in situ during construction and only a new worktop fitted. The full-width sliding folding doors can be opened fully in the summer so the small garden becomes a part of the open plan space and a safe play area.

▶ Project challenges

- To obtain freeholder approval and planning permission for the proposed extension.
- Numerous party wall agreements with other leaseholders and adjoining owners.
- To meet the client's brief on a very tight budget.

Thane Villas

LOCATION: N7, London

PROJECT: Refurbishment, alterations and extension

CLIENT: Private domestic client

ARCHITECT: Marianne Davys Architects

STRUCTURAL ENGINEER: Charles Harris & Partners

PARTY WALL SURVEYOR: James Davidson

CONTRACTOR: WFK Construction

CONSTRUCTION COST: £200,000 + VAT

CONTRACT: JCT Minor Works Building Contract

DATE COMPLETED: 2016

▶ Project brief

The existing house is a three-storey end-of-terrace Victorian house.

The brief included internal alterations and refurbishment, new boiler and hot water storage, underfloor heating on the ground floor, a roof-level bathroom extension to replace the original box room, and a ground-floor extension with open-plan kitchen/dining/living area leading on to the garden, and replacement of windows on the rear elevation. The interior was to be made as light as possible with views out to the garden from all spaces on the ground floor.

▶ Project specifics

The house was in poor condition and with much evidence of historic damp and movement throughout, although it had been underpinned. Floors were not level and walls were not plumb.

A small utility extension to the rear blocked out the sun and the view of the garden, making the interiors at ground-floor level dark.

Part of the ground floor was rebuilt as it was so out of level. The new floors have high levels of insulation and underfloor heating.

The original extension was removed and a large opening formed in the rear wall to provide the new open-plan layout. The new extension spans the full width of the house and provides a spacious dining and living area that opens on to the small south-facing decked garden. A large roof light lets sunlight penetrate into the kitchen area, and from the kitchen island there are views across the dining area into the garden. The front living room retains all the original features and also forms part of the new open-plan space.

The new bathroom at roof level is a welcome and much-needed second bathroom in this four-bedroom family home.

▶ Project challenges

- The original floors, walls, window sills and arches over the windows were not plumb or level, so many decisions involving the client had to be made during the project as to whether to rebuild, improve or leave these elements as part of the history of the building.

- Islington Council imposed many restrictions on the height and setback of the new roof-level bathroom extension, which meant it could only be a small space with a low ceiling.

Larch House

LOCATION: Norfolk

PROJECT: Newbuild house

ARCHITECT: Frost and Frank Architects

STRUCTURAL ENGINEER: Charles Harris & Partners

SERVICES ENGINEER: SGA Consulting

CONTRACTOR: Willow Builders

CONSTRUCTION COST: £248,000 incl. vat

CONTRACT: JCT Minor Works Building Contract with Contractor Design

DATE COMPLETED: 2013

▶ Project brief

The clients are the architects. They had purchased a plot of land and their brief was to build for themselves a new detached house that was highly insulated and easy to run and maintain. The house would be left empty for periods and also used for entertaining family and friends, who would stay in the house.

▶ Project specifics

The new house is detached and has a gross internal area of 115m². The house was built using a prefabricated timber frame with larch cladding, and standing-seam zinc roofing. The house has high levels of thermal insulation and as a result improves on current Building Regulations by 25%. The house uses an air-source heat pump and has underfloor heating. The gardens are an ongoing project.

▶ Project challenges

- To design a contemporary house within a conservative rural setting.

- To use local materials and labour where possible and to design a house that will minimise the consumption of power and water.

- To keep the final cost within £250,000 and approximately £2,000 per m².

- To overcome the lack of local utilities. There was no main drainage, no gas for heating and under-capacity in the local power network. All of this was due to the lack of investment in the privately-owned local utility infrastructure.

Roman Road Gallery

LOCATION: Bethnal Green, London

PROJECT: Refurbishment and extension at ground level

CLIENT: Roman Road Gallery

ARCHITECT: Threefold Architects

STRUCTURAL ENGINEER: Osborne Edwards

QUANTITY SURVEYOR: N/A

CONTRACTOR: Hi-Spec Build (phase 1); Fisk Interiors (phase 2)

CONSTRUCTION COST: £325,000 + VAT

CONTRACT: JCT Intermediate Building Contract with Contractor Design

DATE COMPLETED: 2015

▶ Project brief

The location is a narrow and contextually complex site in the heart of Bethnal Green in London. The building at the front of the site was formerly a commercial premises with an office on the first floor. The building at the rear was a Victorian carpenter's workshop and warehouse with a small walled external courtyard. The brief was unique and challenging: to create a dynamic new contemporary art gallery connected to the curator's house and garden, which are themselves an extension of the gallery space.

▶ Project specifics

After carrying out a feasibility study we decided that the best location for the main public commercial gallery was fronting Roman Road, with its street presence and 'shop window' facade. We located the more private viewing rooms and living spaces towards the back, with bedrooms on the first floor. Strategically, it was decided to carry out the project in two phases: first, the creation

of the commercial gallery to initiate the client's business, and second, the client's private gallery, living spaces and sculpture courtyard.

Ultimately, the finished project completely renovated, reconfigured and knitted together the conjoined but disconnected existing buildings. It also created a new new single-storey extension from contrasting black bricks and glass, which opens the building out on to a brick-paved sculpture courtyard, surrounded by a combination of reclaimed masonry walls and new Corten panels. These were all concealed behind bespoke brick entrance gates.

The flow, character and function of the spaces reflect the link between life and art in the home of the curator-collector. The unprepossessing former building has been transformed into an unexpected double-height gallery space, which opens to the house through sliding screens and on to the courtyard with an expanded flexible space for larger exhibitions, private views and screenings. On the first floor, a folded-steel cantilevered stair leads to the gallery office and private accommodation.

A consistent and restrained palette of materials was used throughout, with crisp bespoke black joinery and metalwork set against the rugged industrial character of the existing buildings.

▶ Project challenges

- To unify disparate buildings of contrasting styles with overlapping public and private programmes.

- To obtain planning and change-of-use consent, for a contemporary new extension within the local conservation area.

- To phase the project, working with two different contractors following on from each other.

- The solid folded-steel cantilevered stair was made and delivered off site, which required careful handling to avoid damaging the powder-coated finish.

- The removal of the floor to create a double-height gallery space created a complex structural bracing solution that had to be hidden within the structure of the internal walls.

ENDNOTES

1   Source: RIBA

2   *See Further Reading*

3   http://www.arb.org.uk/

4   https://www.architecture.com/

5   Source: RIBA Handbook of Practice Management

6   https://www.architecture.com/RIBAMembership/.../FeesToolkit/FeesToolkit.aspx

7   *See page 75 for full list of legislation.*

8   http://www.arb.org.uk/

9   http://www.ribabookshops.com/item/handbook-of-practice-management-9th-edition/80465/

10 Solicitors.lawsociety.org.uk/

11 See the list of employment-related legislation on page 115–116.

12 RIBA Plan of Work: available online from www.architecture.com

13 Traditional procurement: out to tender at Stage 4 when design is complete.

14 www.arb.org.uk/architects-code

15 https://www.architecture.com/RIBA/Professionalsupport/Professionalstandards/CodeOfConduct.aspx

16 http://www.ribabookshops.com/item/a-guide-to-letter-contracts-for-very-small-projects-surveys-and-reports-third-edition/77926/

17 http://www.cdm-2015-regulations.co.uk/

18 www.hse.gov.uk/pUbns/priced/l153.pdf
    Nicholas Jamieson, *Good Practice Guide: Inspecting Works*, 2nd edition (London: RIBA, 2009).

19 www.planningportal.co.uk

20 www.ribabookshops.com/riba-good-practice-guide-series

21 www.legislation.gov.uk

FURTHER READING

Association for Project Safety, *Principal Designer's Handbook: Guide to the CDM 2015 Regulations* (London: RIBA, 2016) Helen Elias, *Good Practice Guide: Marketing Your Practice* (London: RIBA, 2010)

Bryan Spain, *Spon's House Improvement Price Book* (London: Taylor & Francis, 2009)

Comprehensive Building Price Book (BCIS, 2017)

Construction (Design and Management) Regulations 2015: Guidance on Regulations (Health and Safety Executive, 2015) Nicholas Jamieson, *Good Practice Guide: Inspecting Works* (London: RIBA, 2009)

Helen Elias, *Good Practice Guide: Marketing Your Practice* (London: RIBA, 2010)

Nicholas Jamieson, *Good Practice Guide: Inspecting Works* (London: RIBA, 2009)

Nigel Ostime, *A Commercial Client's Guide to Engaging an Architect* (London: RIBA, 2017)

Nigel Ostime, *A Domestic Client's Guide to Engaging an Architect* (London: RIBA, 2017)

Nigel Ostime, *Handbook of Practice Management*, 9th edition, (London: RIBA, 2013)

Nigel Ostime, *RIBA Job Book*, 9th edition, (London: RIBA, 2013)

Nigel Ostime, *Small Projects Handbook*, 1st edition (London: RIBA, 2014)

Paul Hyatt, *In Practice* (EMAP Business Communications, 2000)

Robert Klaschka, *BIM in Small Practices: Illustrated Case Studies* (London: RIBA, 2014)

Roland Phillips, *Good Practice Guide: Fee Management* (London: RIBA, 2009)

Sara Williams, *The Financial Times Guide to Business Start Up* (London: FT Publishing, 2015)

Simon Foxell, *Starting a Practice: A Plan of Work*, 2nd edition, (London: RIBA, 2015)

V.B. Johnson, *Laxton's SMM Building Price Book 2017* (Laxton's, 2017)

Web resources

Architects Registration Board (ARB): www.arb.org.uk

Companies House: www.gov.uk/government/organisations/companies-house

Royal Institute of British Architects (RIBA): www.architecture.com

    Department for Business, Energy and Industrial Strategy: https://www.gov.uk/government/organisations/department-for-business-energy-and-industrial-strategy

    GOV.UK Set up a business: www.gov.uk/starting-up-a-business

    GOV.UK Get help and support for your business: www.gov.uk/business-support-helpline

    GOV.UK Set up a private limited company: www.gov.uk/business-legal-structures/limited-company

    Health and Safety Executive (HSE): www.hse.gov.uk

    HM Revenue and Customs: https://online.hmrc.gov.uk/

    Legislation: www.legislation.gov.uk

    The Pensions Regulator: www.thepensionregulator.gov.uk

RIBA Insurance Agency: www.architectspi.com

Awards for small projects

AJ Small Projects Prize

RIBA House of the Year

RIBA National Awards

RIBA Regional Awards

Stephen Lawrence Prize

Codes

ARB: Architects Code: Standards of Conduct and Practice

RIBA: Code of Professional Conduct

Legislation

List of some of the more important Acts, regulations and codes of practice. A full description of Acts and regulations, and details of current updates, can be checked online on the government legislation website.[21]

PLANNING, DESIGN AND CONSTRUCTION

Building Act 1984

Building Regulations 2010

Community Infrastructure Levy Regulation 2010

Construction (Design & Management) Regulations 2015 (CDM 2015)

Control of Asbestos Regulations 2012

Copyright, Designs and Patents Act 1988

Data Protection Act 1998

Defective Premises Act 1972

General Permitted Development (England) Order *2015*

Housing Acts 1996, 2004

Housing Grants, Construction and Regeneration Act 1996

Localism Act 2011

National Planning Policy Framework 2012

Party Wall etc. Act 1996

Planning and Energy Act 2008

Planning (Listed Buildings and Conservation Areas) Act 1990

Site Waste Management Plan Regulations 2008

The Building (Amendment) Regulations 2016

Town and Country Planning Act 1990

HEALTH AND SAFETY

Health and Safety at Work Act 1974

Health and Safety (Display Screen Equipment) Regulations 1992

Health and Safety (First-Aid) Regulations 1981

Health and Safety (Offences) Act 2008

Management of Health and Safety at Work Regulations 1999

Manual Handling Operations Regulations 1992

Personal Protective Equipment at Work Regulations 2002

Provision and Use of Work Equipment Regulations 1998

Regulatory Reform (Fire Safety) Order 2005

Workplace (Health and Safety and Welfare) Regulations 1992

BUSINESS

Cancellation of Contracts Made in a Consumer's Home or Place of Work etc. Regulations 2008

Companies Act 2006

Competition Act 1998

Consumer Contracts Regulations 2013

Consumer Protection Act 1987

Consumer Rights Act 2015

Contracts (Rights of Third Parties) Act 1999

Late Payment of Commercial Debts (Interest) Act 1998, amended and supplemented by the Late Payment of Commercial Debt Regulations 2002

Supply of Goods and Services Act 1982

The Provision of Services Regulations 2009

Unfair Contract Terms Act 1997

Unfair Contract Terms Act 1997, 2015

Unfair Terms in Consumer Contracts Regulations 1999

Unfair Trading Regulations 2008

EMPLOYMENT

Agency Workers Directive and Regulations 2010

Architects Act 1997

Bribery Act 2010

Employment Act 2008

Employers' Liability (Compulsory Insurance) Act 1969 and Regulations 1998

Employment Relations Act 1999

Employment Rights Act 1996

Equality Act 2010

Human Rights Act 1998

National Minimum Wage Act 1998

Pensions Act 2014

Race Relations Act 1976

Working Time Directive 2013

SUSTAINABILITY

EU LEGISLATION:

Energy Efficiency Directive 2012 (EED)

Energy Performance of Buildings Directive (EPBD)

European 20-20-20 Targets

UK LEGISLATION:

Building Regulations:

     D – Toxic substances

     F – Ventilation

     G – Reduction of water consumption

     L – Conservation of fuel and power

Carbon Plan 2011

Carbon Reduction Commitment (CRC) Energy Efficiency Scheme 2014

Climate Change Act 2008

Climate Change and Sustainable Energy Act 2006

Energy Acts 2008, 2011–2013

Energy Efficiency Regulations 2015

Environment Act 1995

Feed-In Tariffs (FITs) 2016

Green Energy Act 2009

Low Carbon Construction Action Plan 2011

Renewable Heat Incentive (RHI) 2016

UK Renewable Energy Strategy (NPPF) 2009

IMAGE CREDITS

Mark Mc Cullough / Bursar   210 – 211

Tim Crocker / David Fraser   212 – 213

Cat Vinton / Alex and Jill Mackay   214 – 215

Tim Crocker / Marianne Davys   216 – 217

Tim Crocker / Nicky de Bono   218 – 219

Dan Graham / Michelle Lovric   220 – 221

Tim Crocker / Robbie Morton   222 – 223

Ben Rice / Clare Donald   224 – 225

Emma Chapman, Dan O Neill, Herbert Muller / Georgina Frank   226 – 227

Threefold Architects   228 – 229

INDEX